THE POWER OF 10
Rapid Revenue Strategies to Scale Your Business

Jason Miller
Shelby Jo Long
Michael Sipe
Kara James
Mike Jackson
Joel Phillips
Joe Trujillo
Michael Owens
Will Black
Chris O'Byrne

Copyright 2021 Strategic Advisor Board

ALL RIGHTS RESERVED. This book contains material protected under International and Federal Copyright Laws and Treaties. Any unauthorized reprint or use of this material is prohibited. No part of this book may be reproduced or transmitted in any form or by any means, electronic or mechanical, including photocopying, recording, or by any information storage and retrieval system, without express written permission from the author/publisher.

ISBN: 978-1-64184-748-3 (hardback)
ISBN: 978-1-64184-748-3 (paperback)
ISBN: 978-1-64184-749-0 (ebook)

TABLE OF CONTENTS

Introduction v

Foreword ix

Chapter 1   Leadership 1

Chapter 2   Connection 9

Chapter 3   Creativity & Innovation 21

Chapter 4   Connection 28

Chapter 5   Adaptation 40

Chapter 6   Communication 46

Chapter 7   Fulfillment 58

Chapter 8   Relationships 69

Chapter 9   Culture 80

Chapter 10   Mindset 91

Conclusion 101

INTRODUCTION

Foundation. Strategy. Partnership. Impact.

Any company can increase its profits in three ways. First, the company can increase its sales and revenues while maintaining its current costs. Second, the company can decrease its costs, maintaining its current sales and revenue. Third, the company can do something else altogether, where one or both of the first two are possible. As the president of your own company, you have all three options.

Foundation of the Strategic Advisor Board

In 2016, I had a vision of creating a company that could help small businesses grow and thrive. I didn't want to disable them with fees before we even got started, and I also wanted businesses to keep the revenue they had already generated on their own. But I wanted to help businesses grow and take a larger piece of the marketplace. My vision was to be the opposite of the huge consulting firms and create custom solutions that resulted in Rapid Revenue for small businesses. We wouldn't get paid unless we helped create a result. Most said I was crazy and that it would never work. I continued the course, and we have helped hundreds of companies shift and pivot and grow.

The Strategic Advisor Board was forged out of the sheer desire to be different, to go left when everyone else was going right. To disrupt the market and shift the "consulting model" into a more streamlined company that helps small businesses get results. The focus is on the business, the immediate needs of the business in its stage of development, and the long-term strategy to create robust growth within the company. I surround myself with experts in other areas of business so we can provide the best solutions for our clients. The best part is that we have a trusted network of business service providers under the Strategic Advisory Board (SAB) umbrella to fulfill the steps in the strategy. The SAB is your business growth authority and solutions resource center.

Our reason is very simple. We have all been through the yo-yo of business ownership. My design allows us to help business owners finally put down the yo-yo and surround themselves with ten professional working CEOs who have been there and done that. Who have gone through the challenges of ownership and came out the other side successful.

The Power of 10

The Strategic Advisor Board (SAB) is one of a kind in the marketplace. Ten CEOs in the SAB are powerful leaders in their own business brought together under one umbrella to provide the best growth strategy and path for small businesses. The collective experience in the SAB established their business growth model in many different interactions with their clients. Not only does the SAB identify a comprehensive growth strategy for businesses, but we also partner with the business owners to execute the strategy through the short-term strategy and the long-term goals. The SAB is focused on custom solutions and strong relationships.

The power of the SAB is in the diversity in the background and approach within the board. The differing backgrounds of the board members enable the strategies to be articulated for businesses at any stage, but in particular, those businesses that have grown and are sustainable and ready to begin reaching a larger audience, engaging more clients in their business, and are ready to create additional streams of revenue in their business. An all-inclusive strategy map adjusts with the needs of each business to grow and scale the movement of the marketplace. The additional power of the SAB comes from the network of trusted partners to help businesses execute the strategy. With over 55 referral partners in the SAB, the guesswork is taken out of the planning and how to implement the solutions.

Rapid Revenue and Results Model

The Rapid Revenue and Results model acts like a model airplane. There is your vision of the completed product, a clearly articulated, step-by-step process to help you achieve that vision, all of the necessary pieces of the model, the tools needed to put together the pieces, and the glue that holds everything together to finally complete the product.

The SAB acts in a similar way. The SAB creates a unique vision in our partnership with the affiliated business. That framework serves as the guiding path for a business to follow. Then the step-by-step process to generate quick revenue to pay for their next stage of growth. Next, we implement the strategies to help achieve that vision. We use our trusted toolbox/network of trusted service providers to provide the necessary connections to implement the strategies. The glue is the consistent interaction with the SAB board members in our partnership to ensure we are moving your business to the next level. We copilot the strategies with you to adapt to the changing conditions in the marketplace and ensure the business's success.

The long-term strategy architecture serves as the roadmap for the business that focuses on a lasting foundation and community. We explore strategies of how to best engage your ideal client, create a consistent base of referral partners, explore multiple revenue streams in your business, and help create your exit strategy for when you are ready to depart the business.

FOREWORD

SYSTEMS DRIVE PRODUCTIVITY AND GROWTH

The Strategic Advisor Board, like many other powerful businesses, is a well-constructed system. A system consists of many independent parties working together simultaneously yet all interconnected to produce a result greater than what any one person in the system could achieve. A system is not merely a sum of all of the parties working together; the group will take on a life of its own. This idea is the philosophy behind the Strategic Advisor Board. It was brought to life when Jason brought the ten board members together to bring their individual expertise to the table, but when all the members collectively strategize together, the potential is immeasurable.

When a group of individuals is organized in an interdependent way, they perform their own individual tasks to the greatest of their abilities, yet it contributes to the overall performance and success of the organization. Marketing, finance, operations, distribution, customer relations, and team management all have a unique function for creating success in the business. If one of those departments disappears or is not functioning as expected, every other operation in the business environment is affected.

All businesses became acutely aware of this interdependence when the pandemic began to affect our economy in the spring of 2020. Businesses that relied on face-to-face interaction, particularly retail and restaurants, were significantly.

Every business becomes more efficient when its operations are systematized. When predictable systems are developed and implemented within a work environment, work becomes more efficient and productive. This efficiency leads to higher profits for the business in addition to creating a foundation for your business to grow.

These systems become replicable and predictable within the business environment. It becomes easier to create those processes when the business expands its production and capacity. There is consistency of the business brand across all channels.

This is critical for businesses that are considering expanding their capacity. Think about your average coffee shop that wants to open another location. Operations need to be consistent and efficient, there need to be consistent standards of production and execution, and customer service expectations need to be consistent. This replication and consistency are key for business success as they continue to grow and expand.

Even if a business is not considering a franchise or alternate location for business growth, systems and processes are still essential for the business to create standards as other changes begin to affect the business operations. For example, if there is some employee turnover and there are new employees coming into the business environment, a system consistency will create an easier transition. A consistent onboarding process that trains new employees to perform in the expectations of those roles they are being hired for, allows for minimal disruption in the other business operations. Minimized disruptions allow a business to keep its production pace moving forward at expected levels. Businesses can maintain their operational efficiency, serve customers at the highest capacity, and ensure there is no disruption.

The philosophy and the function of the Strategic Advisor Board are centered on this idea of interdependence. Not only do we have ten expert advisors who direct the strategy for small businesses to grow and scale, but we operate as an interdependent network as a partner. Not only does the SAB partner with the businesses to create custom paths forward for each business, but we have a trusted network of business service providers to help implement this direction before business. We help create a connection and growth plan for the business that sets us apart from all other consulting and coaching firms in the business coaching industry.

1
LEADERSHIP

About

Jason Miller is the founder and CEO of the Strategic Advisor Board. He is an author, speaker, mentor, veteran, business strategist, and leader. Leadership is, arguably, the most important aspect of any business. Jason has been active in every C-Suite position and is the current CEO of three successful companies, including the Strategic Advisor Board. Since 2001, Jason has built, owned, sold, and operated over ten companies. Aside from the Strategic Advisor Board, he also currently runs and operates Miller & Company, as well as other companies with multiple brands to include a full-service marketing agency and a government contracting branch where educational services and material contracts are provided to multiple agencies of the United States government.

Jason and his wife, Erika, spent a combined twenty-five years in service to their country in the United States military while simultaneously growing and scaling multiple businesses.

They were able to set their businesses on autopilot with the correct staffing and systems. Jason feels passionately about helping other business owners and CEOs succeed and enjoy their business. He has mentored thousands of people over the last twenty-plus years.

Jason is a published author in the business world. He donates all of his book sales to Homes for Heroes, which has played a major part in building homes for Wounded Warriors. His four published books have been featured worldwide on Amazon and Barnes & Noble. Together, he and Erika wrote *Patriots to Business*, which offers business strategies to help entrepreneurs be successful. Jason has a specialty in helping businesses create a passive system of income. Following that, he helps business owners navigate the rough waters of growing and scaling their company in sequence. Aside from hypergrowth and hyperscaling, Jason specializes in strategic and operational implementation as well as micro-pivots.

Currently, Jason, Erika, and his four children reside in Boulder, Colorado, in the beautiful Rocky Mountains, where they run and operate their main company headquarters. If you need help creating a system for growth and scaling your business, Jason and the rest of the Strategic Advisor Board are here to help. With such a successful background in the business world and proof that Jason's system works, your business is guaranteed to grow. As part of the Strategic Advisor Board, Jason wants to see you and your business succeed. He wants you to have time to enjoy your business. He wants your business plan to support your life plan. With the help of the Strategic Advisor Board, you can become the leader your business needs.

WHAT IS GOOD LEADERSHIP?

Many people sit around and talk about being free of life's hustle and chaos. Many are in love with the dream of being the leader, or by definition, the "protector" of their own lives and what they do. Here is a fact: most will never achieve it. It should be made clear that a leader is not always the one who puts themself in harm's way. Often, the true leader would be considered a normal human being with a relatively common objective. Anyone can call themselves a leader. To be a leader, however, there certainly must be a reason to lead. As a business owner, first be a leader of yourself. Breaking these chains is critical.

Intentions are the glue that holds our lives together. It is our intention that focuses our efforts and aligns us in a singular direction. Being a leader in your own life follows the same simple concept. If you have intention, you have a place to go and a reason to lead yourself and others. In becoming a leader in your own life, start by finding your own intention. Ask yourself this question: "What am I intending in my life?" Find the answer to that, and then you will have the reason you need to lead yourself and your company to success.

When you accept complete responsibility for your life, you begin to view yourself as self-employed, no matter who signs your paycheck. You are the president of your own personal service corporation, the CEO leading a company with one employee: you. You begin to see yourself as responsible for selling one product, your personal services, in a competitive marketplace. You begin to see yourself as completely responsible for every element of your work—for production, quality control, training, development, communication, strategy, productivity improvement, and finances. Refuse to make excuses, and instead, make progress.

Self-leadership does not blindly disregard the objective of the organization, whether this is your own company or a partnership you have with others. It simply means finding what is important to you and applying your best skills and attributes to anything you take on. Effective self-leadership involves achieving an equilibrium between focusing on the cohesiveness of a work group or organization and focusing on the value and identity of each individual employee. Thus, self-leadership does not require entirely autonomous behavior without regard to the team or organization. Nor does it require that the identity and value of each individual employee be entirely put aside in favor of the work group or organization. Rather, an effective self-leadership perspective would encourage individuals to find their own personal identity and mode of contribution as part of an establishment, a group, or an organization that produces synergistic performance.

The last thing readers need to focus on is where they sit in their boardroom of life. Imagine your life is the product, the grand creation of intention and design. In order to enable its success and fulfillment in the marketplace of your mind, it has to be planned with much simplicity, desirability, and usefulness. Once you have settled on what this life should look like, you should promote yourself immediately. You are and always should be the Chief Executive Officer in your own life and company. Your life is the company, and you need to lead it so that it can grow and develop. Remember, you can always change directions and seek new opportunities, and you should always be investing back into yourself. Take charge of your life and become that leader and self-employed CEO that you know exists deep inside! Embrace it and, most of all, dream, believe, and achieve excellence!

Regardless of your business card, leadership is not a title. It's something you earn. It is about more than just ideas and strategy, although those are important. You will not get very far if your employees are not willing to follow you. Yet, too many entrepreneurs take leadership skills for granted. How can you be the kind of leader that brings out the best in people and helps them figure out how to create a new and better future in the midst of unprecedented change? Whether you have natural leadership qualities or you take time learning from mentors, Jason wants to help you capitalize on these qualities so that you can be the best leader for your business.

> *"Leadership is about inspiring people to do things they never thought they could."* – Steve Jobs

There are many innate characteristics associated with leadership. These include ownership, empowerment, caring, and communication, among others. Good leaders must take ownership: ownership of responsibility, ownership of their environment, and ownership of their life. A leader with ownership is a leader with accountability.

True leaders do not allow obstacles to prevent them from taking the next step in their business or in their life. It's important to realize that when taking ownership of responsibility, you do not do everything yourself. Good leaders have mastered the art of delegation. Although someone else is performing the task, you still help shape the outcome. As a leader, you need to know that this is not delegating responsibility to someone else; it is merely delegating a task to a trusted partner in an effort to further community goals together. Lack of trust is delegation's worst enemy. For leaders to build trust, they need to train, coach, and effectively communicate to those within their community. This motivates and empowers people and increases their productivity.

As human beings, we have an innate need and desire to belong. According to Maslow's Hierarchy of Needs, a staple of communication studies, "belonging" is the third stage. Being a great and effective leader requires turning a business into a community. You must inspire self-belief in others. Empowering everyone within your business allows for you and your community to push through comfort zones of where you could be to where you should be.

One of Jason's top priorities within his businesses is making sure those within believe they are part of a community and a family. As a leader, showing care and concern is vital to success. When leaders care for their people, it builds trust, leading to more ownership as a leader and empowerment as a community. Not only does this improve your business's performance, but it allows you to take ownership of and enjoy your life.

Communication is essential to any relationship, and that includes the business sector. It is at the core of effective leadership. Effective and efficient communication builds trust, shows compassion, and emotes respect. It's vital for leaders to participate in both aspects required for effective communication: speaking and listening. Too many leaders often forget that listening is just as, if not more, important as speaking when it comes to communicating. This is especially true with the Strategic Advisor Board. Listening to your business partners and encouraging their input will improve your business overall. Not only does this aid you in understanding others, but it also empowers them, creating trust within your organization.

Understanding what it means to be a good leader is critical to success. Whether you are a natural leader or need some mentoring, the skills and qualities required of a good leader may seem difficult to attain. This is precisely why leadership is earned and not given. As the CEO of the SAB, Jason emanates these qualities and hopes to be able to teach and share them with as many business owners, professionals, and future leaders as possible.

Teamwork

A key part of creating systems that drive productivity and efficiency in your business is clarifying roles within the business. When individuals are focusing on performing their roles during the expectations associated with that role, the operational standards within a business are clear and functional. These definitions make your hiring process more efficient, your operational accountability more distinct, and you lay the foundation for working with a great business culture. You balance the product and processes of your business. You lay the foundation for satisfied employees and customers, which will continue to drive people to your business.

Roles in a business emerge through necessity. When businesses reflect upon their past performance to identify the most efficient way to achieve the processes that best create the product or service, that is the opportunity to create operational efficiency. Documentation of that process helps clarify the roles and expectations that need to be fulfilled to create consistency in the business. This replication of operational standards allows for maximum efficiency in an organization.

When there is a clear definition of the role, the execution of that role in a business helps drive the culture in the business. The culture in a business emerges with the personalities and the experience of the employee interacting with the roles and expectations of the position. The team structure allows for creative solutions and innovative strategies. Employees can perform the role within the business with a method that is best suited for their own working process. This allows for an employee to have more agency in their work, and they will be more committed to the product.

In engaging the Strategic Advisor Board's professional knowledge, you will surpass the superficial client relationships of competitors and build a deep, trusting, long-lasting relationship with clients that will keep them coming back and referring you to their friends, family, and network. Your impact will increase exponentially with a focus on efficient systems and execution standards from the team in your business. This is the magic of the Strategic Advisor Board. We act as a team and grow as a team. The result we achieve is exponential growth in profit and CEO business satisfaction.

As part of the Strategic Advisor Board, Jason helps develop unique growth and scaling strategies for long-term success. Being a good leader and assigning roles within your team is key to creating a community within your business, but the ability to systematically grow and scale your community is how to compete in this market. The Strategic Advisor Board will help you to understand your business's target audience, including their demographics and psychographics, as well as how to drive traffic toward your organization. Once those steps are achieved, the SAB will be your guide in engaging potential clients and persuading them to understand the solution to their problems is you.

The Strategic Advisor Board is here to help you navigate the multifaceted and complex challenges that obstruct the growth and scaling of your business. Your business will be equipped with the resources and support to focus on enjoying the leadership of your business and of your life. By employing the help of the Strategic Advisor Board and Jason's expertise, your business is guaranteed to increase revenue. By employing the qualities of a good leader and implementing an individualized, long-term success strategy, you can create a competitive advantage. A new and improved growth strategy, as well as a hands-on leader, will gain attention, making clients recognize and remember your business.

2
CONNECTION

About

Shelby Jo Long is an author, speaker, professor, and business strategist that helps businesses grow their brand by developing custom courses. She helps experts, academics, and authors transform their unique ideas and stories into digital programs so they can scale their operations. Shelby's professional background includes 15 years as a professor and intercollegiate debate coach at Rocky Mountain College in Montana. She has taught classes in the communication studies discipline, including business communication, public speaking, small group communication, argumentation and debate, persuasion, and organizational communication. Shelby's involvement with debate has enabled her to travel around the United States and the world. In addition to conducting international communication and debate seminars in New York City, she has been involved in seminars in Mexico, Bosnia, Ireland, and Morocco. Furthermore, she has mentored students on trips across the United States and various countries for international debate competitions.

In Shelby's business strategist and consulting work, she has led business culture and communication training for state-level and private organizations. She has also been invited to speak at women's conferences, chamber events, and real estate conferences about leadership, organizational culture, and branding. Her communication and advocacy backdrop gives a unique perspective on how a business conveys its message to its audiences.

Shelby, along with her husband Tony and children Ava and Emmett, lives in Billings, Montana. Her family loves spending time outdoors and visiting their family in Missoula, Montana, and Central Idaho. Her book, *I See Your Genius: Take Your Idea to Income,* is forthcoming.

Shelby's extensive experience has culminated with expertise in her own personal brand: the customer acquisition process. Client generation is critical to any business. Businesses need clients to survive, and it is impossible to think about growth unless the business expands its client base. Client generation does not happen without communication. When business owners and employees understand the needs and communication habits of clients, there is a higher potential for a business transaction.

Target Markets

In an age where anyone can find any product or service anywhere in the world, small businesses are faced with the challenge of competing with both their local market and a worldwide online market. With limited resources compared to their online competitors, how can entrepreneurs develop a strong market advantage? By targeting the needs of certain markets and creating relationships with clients, small businesses will continually add value. Entrepreneurs can create a competitive advantage.

If you don't develop a strategy for the target audience for your product, there's a risk of having a low return on investment from marketing dollars. You also spend more time and resources trying to attract clients, which takes time. There are a few actions to take in a business to help create that connection with your ideal client. This connection helps your business create a relationship with clients that will boost your market for referral and return services.

First, clarify your ideal client. Who is the best match for your business? To understand and categorize audience needs, refer to specific information, such as demographics (the age, gender, occupation, income, education, and other quantifiable characteristics of the people you're trying to persuade) and psychographics (personality, attitudes, lifestyle, and other psychological characteristics). When analyzing the ideal client, take into account their cultural expectations and practices so that one doesn't undermine their persuasive message by using an inappropriate appeal or by organizing a message in a way that seems unfamiliar or uncomfortable to readers.

Basic demographic questions are critical. Is the ideal audience male or female? Generation Z or Generation X? Married or single? These demographic questions will then inform the way that one chooses to communicate and market to the audience they will serve.

An entrepreneur should also explore the psychographic descriptors of the ideal audience. What attitudes, behaviors, and interests does the ideal audience have? These questions can further inform where a business could network to find clients and which channels to use to sell their service or product most effectively.

Second, become a resource for your clients. How does your business deliver results for your clients? Thinking about your clients and their needs will guide your message. Clients are searching for a quality product or a valuable service. Be prepared to outline the benefits of your service to the clients. When a client understands these benefits, they will be more loyal to a business.

Intentional communication is critical to developing an extended relationship with clients. When engaging a client base, for instance, by providing additional information on a regular basis, an entrepreneur continues to participate in the growth of their business. One can also engage clients with loyalty programs or incentives for referrals. When an entrepreneur focuses on the relationships with their clients, they will continue to strengthen their business foundation and elevate their business above the competition.

Third, differentiate yourself from your competitors. How can a business set itself apart from others? When an entrepreneur understands the competition, they can develop a better idea of how their business can provide a unique offering to a target audience or client. Do a deep analysis of local competition to identify ways to differentiate your business. Think of incentives, promotions, or customer relation strategies that can be used to set your business apart from others.

These unique strategies will begin to elevate your business above the competition because you have something valuable to offer in your service. These strategies act as a form of brand cultivation so clients will recognize and remember your business.

While this online era has been challenging for small businesses, consumer behavior has not changed much within the online marketplace. People still spend money when and where they trust the provider. Consumers will stay loyal to businesses when they appreciate the service and the product.

Traffic

When it comes to running a business, traffic is essential. Traffic is when people learn about your business. In order to begin a relationship with your clients, there must be an initial meeting. Even if you meet potential clients at a networking event, they will likely visit your social media or website to learn more about you and your business. There are many ways to increase traffic to your digital platforms. The following simple steps will attract leads.

First, create and cultivate your brand. Have a clear focus on what you do, who you serve, and how you engage with clients. Be consistent with your digital presence and communication to create a returning stream of clients. Cultivating your image is important because it not only makes a memorable impression with consumers, it distinguishes yourself from the competition and clarifies what your business offers that makes you the better choice. When engaging with your brand's story, you connect with clients on an emotional level. This opens the possibility for trust and a long-term business relationship.

Second, develop strategic partnerships. Trying to do everything alone in business will quickly become frustrating and overwhelming. Yet, when partnered with another business, the workload is lessened by helping each other to achieve mutual success. Collaborating with similar businesses will also expand reach and multiply leads. Burgeoning entrepreneurs will offer greater innovation, greater value, and better results with strategic partnerships.

Third, create a clear value proposition. We may be in business to serve our own needs, but our potential customers are searching for solutions to their problems. A clear value proposition will best engage and build trust with potential clients when entrepreneurs provide possible solutions to their problems. This value proposition will differentiate your business from the competition and create a solid referral base.

Fourth, select the right media, platforms, or channels. In some situations, various members of an audience might prefer different media for the same message. Some consumers like to do all their car shopping in person, while others prefer to research and browse online. Some clients would prefer promotional emails for products they are interested in, while others hate every marketing email they receive. A single medium of communication might not reach most or all of your audience. Entrepreneurs need to use two or more platforms, such as following up an email campaign with print marketing, for instance. By providing messaging through multiple media, there will be greater reach to connect with more potential clients.

When you select a target market, entrepreneurs will be more successful in driving traffic toward their brand. The long-term customer acquisition process begins once potential clients find a business, understand the value proposition, and connect with the brand.

Engaging the New Consumer

With a specified target market and a plan to drive potential clients toward your business, it is time to engage the client and persuade them that you're the answer to all their problems.

Consumer behavior changed in 2020. While purchases are currently centered on the most basic needs, people are shopping more consciously, buying local, and embracing digital commerce. To manage isolation, consumers are using digital to connect, learn, and play—and they will continue to.

The way in which consumers are responding to the Coronavirus crisis varies. Some are anxious and worried, which fueled the panic-buying of staples and hygiene products. At the other end of the spectrum, consumers remained indifferent to the pandemic and continued their daily habits or business as usual. Entrepreneurs and emerging business owners should understand how their consumers are reacting to crises such as COVID-19 to develop personalized strategies to target each market in a given situation.

To prevent the flood of information consumers are faced with, an entrepreneur can help them by making connections in their business relationships and drawing them in to be part of a community. Here are some tips to successfully engage consumers in an organization.

First, engage your personality in your marketing. One of the biggest advantages of matching your personality to your job is the greater ease of connecting with your colleagues and clients. Consumers trust people much more than products or services. When a consumer knows about the person and brand behind the service, they are more likely to buy. When planning the next piece of content, try to write like you talk, lose the cliches, use lighthearted visuals, and add videos!

Second, be transparent in your business. Customer transparency is a business practice that values corporate honesty and encourages companies to communicate both positive and negative information with their customers. Put plainly, it is a concept that encompasses a value system meant to put the customer first and to present the client with all of the necessary information they need to make an educated purchase. Transparency can be cultivated by clearly articulating what the consumer can expect from a business transaction. The entrepreneurs are responsible for creating a comfortable and trusting atmosphere with potential clients.

Third, discuss the results. What are the direct results of engaging in a business transaction with your business? What are the intangible results? When a client is connected to the larger, core commitment of a business, their referral and return service will increase. Engaging a new type of customer is also an added potential; people begin to trust businesses when they know you are invested in creating solutions for them. Discussing results creates a strong foundation for business return and growth.

Fourth, establish credibility in your messaging. It is important to convey your knowledge in the business without misleading clients. When communicating, use simple language to avoid suspicions of fantastic claims and emotional manipulation. Provide objective evidence for claims and promises. Like the previous tip, what are the direct results of engaging in a business transaction with your business? Is there data or testimonials to share? Display willingness to keep your audience's best interests at the center of your efforts. Remember that the purpose of your business should be to solve a client's problems, not to make money. Finally, whenever possible, try to build credibility before presenting a major proposal. In doing this, clients don't have to evaluate both you and the message simultaneously.

When the potential client has been engaged, it is time to build the relationship. Once the initial connection is made, think about the next stage in the sales process. Cultivate a relationship by understanding the needs of clients and connecting with them. To develop deeper connections, consider Aristotle's modes for persuasion, otherwise known as rhetorical appeals. Stronger relationships result in an increased investment in your business, more transactions with ideal matches, consistent return and referral service, and more clients overall.

In Aristotle's work "Poetics," he said: "Of the modes of persuasion furnished by the spoken word, there are three kinds. The first kind depends on the personal character of the speaker; the second on putting the audience into a certain frame of mind; the third on the proof, or apparent proof, provided by the words of the speech itself."

Aristotle describes how we connect with others when he describes his appeals. The speaker's appeals enable us to build relationships with potential clients. These three methods are ethos, pathos, and logos.

Ethos is an appeal to credibility. Connect with clients by displaying your expertise in the field. When you state your credibility, your clients gain a transparent understanding of your business process, your offer, and your expertise. To help increase the ethos in the sales process, actively showcase tools of credibility online. Online credibility consists of reviews, testimonials, case studies, social media posts, and more. The more expertise, results-driven data, and claims displayed through a third party, the more people will trust your business and overall credibility in your specialty area.

Pathos is an appeal to emotion. Connect with clients using emotional appeals. Point clients toward the benefits of working with you. Humans are emotional beings and seek human connection where experiences are shared. Emotions can play an immense role in sales strategy. However, it needs to be used wisely and combined with ethos and logos. There are four basic emotions that can be effective in marketing: happiness, sadness, fear, and anger. Each will elicit a different response in clients. For this reason, entrepreneurs must be careful with what emotion they evoke in their clients to develop a connection.

Logos is an appeal to logic. Use logic to reason with clients. When a necessary, significant connection between your service and the client is created, the value proposition is complete. This strategy is based on a client's need to justify a purchase. To create a connection with clients, include fact sheets, statistics, or other forms of logical and scientific reasoning. Try creating a "logic sandwich" in marketing. Start with presenting an emotionally charged problem to hook the client's attention, follow it with a logical explanation of how your product can help them, and return to the previously established emotional theme.

Business is about building relationships. Determine the best way to connect with potential clients by thinking about these three Aristocratic methods. Employing these strategies will successfully lead through from client engagement to the acquisition process.

Client Relationships

Finally, ensure that newly created client relationships are maintained. A good client acquisition process will not help grow and sustain business if entrepreneurs are not able to keep clients. Relationships are essential to business. Relationships between clients, employees, and other businesses are necessary for creating and sustaining business. Connections are the source of your business culture. Reliance on this network is needed to sustain and grow your business.

Communication is key in the sales process. There is an important connection between the task of selling and the relationship that is built during a sale. The tension between this task and the relationship between the buyer and seller is critical to a successful transaction. An understanding of the different buyer types and how to adapt communication to these clients will help build trust between you and your client. The trust is central for immediate business, future business, and referrals. Studies vary on the kind of relationships, but there is agreement on a few major themes. The typical buyer personality types fall into four categories: Assertive, Analytical, Amiable, and Artistic.

The assertive client likes to be in control, is competitive, and is goal-oriented. They are less concerned about developing a relationship with the seller and more concerned about the outcome. Be logical, direct, and fact-oriented when speaking to assertive buyers. They will respond to direct statements but will also attempt to drive the conversation. Take control and discuss results and the return on investment with these types of buyers.

An analytical client is thoughtful, comparative, and typically distrustful of salespeople. They like to see the logic behind the purchase. Use facts and examples when selling to an analytical audience. Compare your product or service to competitors and move slower with these personality types. Ask questions and discuss some potential drawbacks to avoid risk. Analytical buyers appreciate the extra attention and thoughtfulness rather than the sales pitch.

An amiable personality is friendly, loyal, and low risk. These customers are primarily concerned with developing a relationship. Seek common ground through small talk and show a general interest with amiable clientele. They are loyal to service providers and salespeople with whom they choose to do business because these clients tend to avoid conflict and negotiation. Showing a personal commitment and attempting to create a relationship will gain business with the amiable client type.

Clients who could be categorized as artistic and expressive are assertive and impulsive. They typically have a short attention span and will make quick decisions. These personality types are fulfilled by relationships as well as accomplishing tasks. Tell stories and discuss experiences with artistic clients because they typically make decisions on the first day. Due to the artistic client's assertiveness, use goal-oriented language to help close the deal.

Adapting your communication to your audience is essential in business. Start to understand your client base and their communication needs to build better relationships, create a returning customer base, and gain more referral business.

As part of the Strategic Advisor Board, Shelby helps develop unique communication strategies for business transactions. The target audience and client traffic are key to marketing and to business, but the ability to communicate with different personality types is how to compete in this market. The Strategic Advisor Board will help you to understand your business's target audience, including their demographics and psychographics, as well as how to drive traffic toward your organization. Once those steps are achieved, the SAB will be your guide in engaging potential clients and persuading them to understand the solution to their problems is you.

The Strategic Advisor Board is here to help you navigate the multifaceted and complex challenges that obstruct the scaling of your business. Growing a business quickly requires special attention to customers' needs, wants, and desires. With Shelby's extensive background in developing a good customer acquisition process, you will be equipped with the resources and support to focus on developing products and communication practices that will fill customer gaps and grow your company.

By employing the help of the Strategic Advisor Board and Shelby's expertise, your business is guaranteed to expand its reach. By targeting the needs of certain markets and creating relationships with clients that continually add value, you can create a competitive advantage. A new and improved form of brand cultivation will gain attention, making clients recognize and remember your business. In engaging the SAB's professional knowledge, you will surpass the superficial client relationships of competitors and build a deep, trusting, long-lasting relationship with clients that will keep them coming back and referring you to their friends, family, and network. Your impact will increase exponentially from where it was before you enlisted the help of the Strategic Advisor Board.

3
CREATIVITY & INNOVATION

About

Michael Sipe is a veteran consultant and executive coach with a passion for helping create abundance in your business and personal life to ensure life is full of purpose and fulfillment. Michael has trained, coached, and mentored thousands of people for more than three decades. He is an engineer, author, pilot, financial planner, and energy coach. Michael acts as the COO of the Strategic Advisor Board, as well as the CEO of other coaching and consulting brands under his company Michael Sipe LLC. He has been an Innovation Director, the Senior Advisor to the DoD Strategic Capabilities Office, and a Master Practitioner in Core Energy Coaching. Michael is also a best-selling author with his current book, *Out of Dad's Box: How to Break Free from Parental Control and Transform Your Life at Any Age*.

Michael has thrived in both military and business endeavors. Having graduated with a versatile systems engineering degree from the US Naval Academy, he has fully understood the intricate linkages that combine to form the comprehensive picture of technological and organizational structures. His unique insight allows him to adapt and excel in disparate professional disciplines. This diverse exposure creates an immense amount of experience. Further, he values his training as a core energy coach most. Michael's training and coaching experience enable him to fully understand someone logically, emotionally, and intuitively to drive them to their full, supernatural potential.

Michael specializes in creating an expansion with an abundance mindset, fostering a workforce that is engaged, enthusiastic, and profitable. He uses his keen intuitiveness to integrate vertical and horizontal business systems that complement a scaled capability for hypergrowth. He has consulted both large multinational capitalization and micro-capitalization companies specializing in turning innovative ideas into marketplace value creation. Michael specializes in creating a workforce that is engaged, caring, and revenue-growing.

Michael aims to create an awareness of why we make the choices we do and how to shift from our limited-belief consciousness to, instead, be incredible about all we pursue in life. He excels in helping small and large business executives achieve increased profitability and personal fulfillment. If you need help shifting to an expansion mindset built on abundance, Michael and the rest of the Strategic Advisor Board can assist in doing the "mental surgery" and shifting mindset energy to one of explosive growth—for your business and personal life.

Michael is a happy husband and father of two. He, his wife, Mary, and their children live in Colorado and Florida to take advantage of both the majestic mountain scenery and Surfside beaches. They love to spend time surfing, snowboarding, and enjoying the great outdoors.

Energy

Creating a culture that is engaged, enthusiastic, and profitable is vital in growing your business's revenue. Michael has a passion for transforming workforce culture into one that allows for business and personal growth. He sees his ability to make connections and inspire employees as his contribution to society.

Michael discovered an organization that focused on "core energy" that teaches awareness and usage of the attitudes individuals and organizations have on any given day. The Institute for Professional Excellence in Coaching developed their Energy Leadership Index, which assesses people's energy, attitudes, and perspectives.

The Energy Leadership Index assessment reveals the specific filters people have developed and how they influence their life. It also uncovers the thinking and perceptions that might be creating stress or holding people back from achieving their goals. Michael's spiritual side resonated with the holographic thinking of logical, emotional, and intuitive intelligence. He became skilled at understanding and explaining the findings of Energy Leadership Index assessments as an Energy Leadership Index practitioner. After all, the ability to achieve success, happiness, and purpose happens when people recognize and release internal challenges and blocks.

Michael found there is often one problem many businesses unknowingly face: an unenergetic workforce. The enthusiasm, or lack thereof, that people have for their jobs is independent of their personalities. People get frustrated when things don't go their way. They want to inspire managers and executives while not getting caught up in every challenge they face, which drains them of their energy. Furthermore, executives often mistakenly demand, threaten, manipulate, drive, incentivize, use willpower and other actions to make people do their jobs. Rather than being a leader, they accidentally become a boss.

Most talented people don't respond well to a demanding and high-supervision environment. Their response is carried with negative energy, specifically catabolic energy. Employees try to power through work or the minimum required. They burn out quickly and can't sustain the drive over more extended periods. In short, they feel victimized. If people feel victimized, they retreat from work and don't offer their talents willingly.

On the other hand, more elevated energy is referred to as anabolic energy. This is where people feel inspired, collaborative, creative, enthusiastic, excited, masterful, joyous, unstoppable, and at peace. Anabolic energy is contagious! It is important to note that positive energy is seen more in start-ups or within teams that are inspired and driven to tackle enormous challenges. As one might guess, anabolic energy is often missing in established businesses and organizations.

Throughout the days or weeks, people cycle and shift through anabolic and catabolic energy levels. Stress is the primary reason energy tends to shift from anabolic to catabolic. Research studies have shown that when leaders bring anabolic energy to a team, group, or business, the likelihood of success increases. Leaders who implement the best practices and instill an anabolic energy environment become consistent change agents achieving new levels of success despite the increasingly complex socio-economic times. Behind the shift to more energetic employees and an increase in business vitality is the connection with people. Michael can help implement an excellent management program that will help bring progress, efficiency, improved performance, and better quality to a business's products and services.

Michael and the rest of the Strategic Advisor Board can energize your workforce culture leading to an increase in revenues. Focusing on decreasing stress and leading your employees in an anabolic energy environment will doubtlessly guide your organization to prosperity.

Manifest Management

When people say they manifested certain behaviors or outcomes into their lives, do you believe them? That by simply believing something will happen to them, something actually will happen? This practice is called the Law of Attraction. Michael felt stuck in his previous occupation, but by employing this practice, he transformed his life into something he enjoys: helping others as an entrepreneur.

There are few recognized universal laws, with the Law of Attraction being the granddaddy of them all. Whatever ideas or beliefs people have are brought into their experience proportionably to the occupancy of thought. On average, people think upwards of 50,000 to 60,000 thoughts per day, with most being subconscious thoughts. If people focus on hate, discontent, and victimhood a significant amount of time, they attract it. Therefore, that's what the universe manifests into their experience.

The Law of Attraction, or LOA, has been around for decades and is primarily focused on individual wants and desires. There are many ways to use LOA for personal benefit. Users of the practice have absolute faith, a conviction that what they desire is already done. The Law of Attraction works.

An important thing to remember is that there is always a consequence of your choices. It is the yin and yang of the universe. Fortunately, LOA exists to help break free and have a consequence for the better. Experts of the practice explain that to ensure the Law of Attraction's application is successful, people need conviction. They need to feel like the task is already complete, that the desire is already done.

A mistake many executives make is controlling employees with a hands-on approach. Think of it as bossing others around rather than leading others. They repel rather than attract when they do that. They need to trust with conviction when they try to manifest for their teams, businesses, or people as executives. To be a manifesting executive, you must pull from the quantum realm of infinite possibilities, the one you most want to experience. Leaders who use the Law of Attraction to benefit their people act as a tide, lifting all boats.

There is a crucial ingredient in manifesting beneficially for others. Your motives can't be ego-based. You can't be doing it for the recognition or promotion of your ego. The practice and manifestation become null and void when you do that. If your ego is asking for the universe's help, then it subconsciously believes it doesn't have it and needs it. That ego-need repels. Check your motives and work to minimize or eliminate the ego drive. Instead, focus on the gist of manifestation. This way, you are more aligned with how LOA operates.

The very nature of the universe is to want to fulfill both individual and group desires. You can demonstrate the manifestation practice as a leader and execute a magnanimous vision that benefits all involved.

As part of the Strategic Advisor Board, Michael helps develop strategies to energize workforce culture for improved efficiency, revenue growth, and to find fulfillment. Michael's higher-level consciousness sees both the hidden opportunities and the potentially disabling activities of a client's business. He passionately champions a client's business, not just for contracted sessions but also after hours—strategizing and brainstorming epiphanies to accelerate a business's growth opportunities. Michael gets to know clients at a deep level to learn how they tick and then formulates significantly transformative approaches unique to that client.

By employing the help of the Strategic Advisor Board and Michael's expertise, your business is guaranteed to improve energy and efficiency. After working with Michael, you will come to fully grasp how to execute a strategy of two to twenty times scalability and growth. You will also come to understand the why of your business, ensuring business longevity. Michael's three-part process (strategy, leadership, and culture) creates solutions to address the most significant challenges to small business scalability.

In engaging the SAB's professional knowledge, you will outmaneuver the superficial company culture of competitors and build a long-lasting relationship with clients and those within your company that will keep them coming back and referring you to their friends, family, and network. Your energy and impact will increase exponentially from where it was before you enlisted the help of Michael and the Strategic Advisor Board.

4
CONNECTION

About

Kara James is a business coach and strategist with a specialty in helping other coaches scale their online businesses by creating irresistible offers that convert to sales. She has a corporate business background going back to the early '90s.

Kara is the owner of the successful coaching business, Pursue and Thrive, LLC. She has helped many coaches in various niches double and even triple their revenue by helping them create different tiered offers to fill their value ladder, which in turn creates a consistent flow of revenue in their businesses month after month. She is also a certified partner with the well-known CRM company, Keap/Infusionsoft.

Kara was voted one of the top 500 entrepreneurs in *Brainz Magazine* for 2020, alongside Kamala Harris and Elon Musk. She is a best-selling author and has certifications in Business and Entrepreneurial Coaching, Digital Marketing, Integrative

Wellness, Life and Motivational Coaching, as well as a "triple threat" certification in Offer Creation, Copywriting and Funnel Building.

Kara is married to her high school sweetheart and is the proud mom of three incredibly talented young adults. She resides in the gorgeous Finger Lakes area of Upstate New York.

What is the Broken Onboarding Process?

Organizations differ in their definition of the employee onboarding process. The process is universal, but the time period of the process, as well as the tasks involved, are unique amongst businesses. Every onboarding process includes the orientation program, the training plan, setting up performance metrics, and a feedback loop.

In short, the employee onboarding process is when a new employee is hired and joins the organization. Some businesses consider the start of this process to be when the employee completes their new hire paperwork and is complete when they are introduced to the organization, while other businesses consider it to start when the hiring manager makes the offer and lasts until the employee starts producing quality work in their role.

Employee onboarding is the process of introducing new employees to the organization's environment and culture. A solid employee onboarding process is necessary to help new hires settle down in their jobs, get to know the organization, obtain clarity in their job objectives, and forge a good relationship with other employees. If the experience fails to live up to expectations, a new hire might regret their decision to accept the job offer. The negative impression left by a poor onboarding process might affect a new hire's perceptions of the employers, give them prejudiced notions about the organization, and ultimately cause them to quit early.

The disadvantages of a broken onboarding process are widespread. It may suggest that leaders do not care about new hires and are disinterested in their success. Every employee wants an organization where they can learn, grow, and flourish. Without that, they will ultimately feel resentful toward the organization and leave. Turnover is proven to be greatly affected by the presence or lack of onboarding. According to a survey conducted by the Aberdeen Group, 86% of new hires decide to stay or leave a company within their first six months, and new employees are 69% more likely to stay longer than three years if they experience a well-structured onboarding process. A high turnover rate means a larger rehiring time, expenses, and a delay in other business plans and development. A broken onboarding process affects the rest of the business.

In order to ensure a successful employee onboarding process, there are many components that need to be understood first.

Group Development

Poor group development is a contributing factor to a broken onboarding process. Not only will being part of a successful group create a sense of belonging for the new hire, but it will also create trust among the new hires and current employees. When team members trust one another, they are more likely to share ideas, collaborate effectively, and make the right decisions for everyone and the project, leading to everyone having a sense of achievement and, as a result, creating an economic benefit for the business. Group development is made up of four stages: forming, storming, norming, and performing.

Forming is the reason that we join groups. This stage can be described as a time period when the group is just starting to come together and is usually filled with anxiety, uncertainty, and apprehension. Everyone in the workplace will be put into a group; whether it is something like the accounting department, a group put together to create a promotional campaign, or a committee that creates rules and regulations to help the workplace.

The next stage is storming, which is marked by primary tension and secondary tension. Primary tension is the initial anxiety of joining a group. Small talk, politeness, uneasiness, feeling embarrassed, and shyness are all primary tensions. Secondary tension comes when the group makes decisions. Conflict is created because of role struggles, disagreements over ideas, and differences in personalities. It is an awkward moment in the group development process, and a group will be stuck in this stage if norming does not occur, as described below.

Norming is vital to achieve group goals, regulate behavior in the group, and determine the process of a group. There are two types of norms: explicit and implicit. Explicit norms are written rules that identify acceptable behavior. Wearing a uniform, answering the phone a certain way, and being in the office at a certain time are all examples of explicit norms. On the contrary, implicit norms are rules of respect and decorum within a group that develops from interaction. They are influenced by cultural and societal standards. Not interrupting others while they are speaking, using workplace-appropriate language, and completing work to the best of your ability are all examples of implicit norms. By following the norms set by the group members, success is guaranteed to a group.

Finally, the last stage of group development is performing. In this stage, the group is completing the task that they were formed to do. Group members are motivated to work together as a cohesive group, and they find ways to solve lingering or new problems. Group morale and loyalty are high, and the group is characterized by trust, experience, compatibility, and organization. The task will be completed, and the group will be a success.

How does group development affect the onboarding process? Not only does being a part of a successful group help a new hire to feel wanted and comfortable in the workplace, but a group can even be formed for the specific purpose of helping the onboarding process. This group can ensure new hires feel welcomed with small gestures like being formally introduced to the current employees, a friendly note from their manager, information to make their first day successful like how to use the office phones and computers, as well as providing them with the necessary login information, a virtual or physical copy of the employee handbook, and other details about the new hire's department and job responsibilities.

The Flow of Communication in the Workplace

Having a group to help with the flow of communication will aid new hires in understanding the organization's flow of communication. Being able to communicate effectively across an organization, from the highest levels to the lowest levels, creates a workplace culture that promotes productivity and efficiency. Employees are better able to understand each other, which increases office morale and unity. There are five main types of communication flow within an organization: downward, upward, lateral, diagonal, and external.

Downward communication is communication that flows down from the higher levels of an organization to the lower levels, or down the chain of command. This type of communication transmits work-related information to lower-level employees, which helps them meet the expectations that have been set by their superiors. Managers use this communication to give feedback on an employee's performance, relay instructions, provide understanding for an employee's job, as well as the role it plays in the organization, and communicate the vision and mission of the organization to employees.

Upward communication flows from the lower levels of an organization to the higher levels, which helps relay the effectiveness of downward communication and allows employees to convey their opinions and ideas. Upward communication gives employees a voice within the organization, allowing them to share their grievances, opinions, and ideas, and allows for managers to work out any issues and keep the workplace tension-free. When effectively utilized, upward communication creates more loyal and committed employees because they feel like they can have ownership and a voice in the organization.

Lateral communication takes place at the same level of hierarchy within an organization and is used to save time, facilitate the coordination of tasks, facilitate cooperation among employees, solve problems within the organization, share information, and resolve conflicts. When lateral communication is being used effectively, it creates camaraderie and builds rapport with coworkers. Many times this flow of communication brings coworkers closer because it provides them with emotional and social assistance in the office.

Diagonal communication exists when a manager works with employees from another department or workgroup. This is utilized in instances when a project spans multiple departments or a manager is creating a training module and works with employees from various departments to ensure that the training is accurate, for instance. Effective diagonal communication leads to uniformity across an organization in branding, vision, mission, and values, as well as helps prevent any miscommunication that may occur through the communication chain.

Finally, external communication exists between a manager and an external group such as vendors, suppliers, banks, and the like. This communication helps to ensure that the organization has all that it needs to be able to function properly.

While it may seem redundant, understanding the flow of communication in a new hire's organization will help the new hire feel more comfortable. They will know exactly who to refer to when a problem arises, and they will be integrated into the unfamiliar environment easily and quickly.

Introducing a New Hire to Workplace Culture

Culture is the environment that surrounds us all the time. It differs from group to group and will be new and unfamiliar to new hires in the onboarding process. Workplace culture can be described as the shared values, belief systems, attitudes, and the set of assumptions that a workplace shares. This is shaped by individual upbringing and is specific to a social and cultural context. However, in the workplace, leadership and business strategy influences the workplace culture to a great degree. A positive workplace culture improves teamwork, raises employee morale, increases productivity, efficiency, and enhances employee retention. Job satisfaction, collaboration, and work performance are all enhanced. Most importantly, a positive work environment reduces employee stress.

The employee onboarding process extends long after the new hire's first day. To prevent having a broken onboarding process, business leaders need to be working consistently to enhance workplace culture. First, a clear mission and core values need to be established. It is important to have a set of clear organizational values that are communicated effectively and discussed with all of the employees so that everyone feels like part of the team. It is the commitment that an organization makes to certain policies and actions, like going green or being diverse and inclusive to all groups. It is not enough to state this in the mission statement, brand story, or in promotional material. This is all performative action, but it is crucial that genuine actions are regularly taken so that employees feel a personal responsibility toward these values. This will ensure your staff can take pride in your core values and bring them to fruition in their individual roles. Positive attitudes and positive actions make for a positive workplace culture.

Secondly, fostering collaboration in the workplace makes for a positive culture that will aid in creating a successful onboarding process. An organization that encourages teamwork, as well as open and honest communication, is crucial to creating a positive culture. Open communication also means that regular checkups are made to evaluate how people are interacting with each other, that a feedback loop is created, and opportunities for social interaction are enabled. Opportunities for team members to nurture and foster connections outside of work are important, as well as continued learning opportunities to enable team members to assess unconscious and implicit biases that can impact their interactions with other employees. A workplace where everyone is comfortable and feels needed makes for a positive culture.

Finally, try creating clear goals and rewards for employees to foster a positive workplace culture and help new hires adjust to the organization. Motivated and engaged employees are the result of a workplace that treats each member of the team equally, with respect, and has clear goals that they can work toward. Having a transparent policy for progression and promotion offers the staff an opportunity to measure their performance and success. Measurable performance indicators foster healthy competition, but an honest policy statement helps avoid negative feelings and resentment among team members. When goals are positively reinforced, and achievements are celebrated, it leads to employees feeling valued and creates a positive workplace environment.

By following the previous tips, new hires will feel welcome and comfortable in their new position and will want to stay at the organization, lowering the turnover rate and bettering its reputation. Finally, the topic of inclusion absolutely needs to be addressed to create a successful onboarding process.

Creating an Environment of Inclusion and Respect

Inclusion is not only important in the onboarding process because of the happy feeling it creates. It also impacts innovation, employee engagement, retention, and recruiting, all of which have the potential to improve a business. Most importantly, an inclusive and diverse onboarding process sets each employee up for success, regardless of their gender, race, ethnicity, experience, or personality. Once introduced to the organization, employees should feel that they made the right decision to join the business, including a sense of belonging and purpose in their position.

First, understanding the societal expectations of gender is vital. Men have a certain expectation of behavior. In the workplace, they must be powerful, aggressive, dominant, competitive, problem-solvers, direct, and focused. Besides these nonverbal behaviors, men are expected to have a certain body language. They are supposed to make use of space, be open, and employ face-to-face communication.

Women also have a certain expectation of behavior. In the workplace, they must be submissive, quiet, passive, emotional, and conflict-avoidant. Besides these nonverbal behaviors, women are expected to have a certain body language. Society may suggest women should be closed off and take up as little physical space as possible. The majority of women also, unfortunately, face obstacles such as unequal pay and glass ceilings. Despite the advances made in the business world, a wage gap still exists between men and women. Although the wage gap has certainly improved, there are still changes that can be made to empower women the same way men are empowered. Creating a successful employee onboarding process starts in the workplace with a diverse and inclusive business.

To achieve this, the best tip and practice is to be aware of the gender difference in the workplace. Additionally, recognize that these differences in verbal and nonverbal communication are not established rules of behavior. Adapt your communication to your audience. Be respectful of the differences in gender amongst employees in your workplace. Be aware of stereotypes and biases in order to not offend coworkers. Most importantly, be an active audience member and listener. Consult your employees to learn how to be a more inclusive workplace and make changes that will help both men and women. If a respectful environment is already developed in the workplace, then the employee onboarding process will be more successful.

Similarly, respect for racial and ethnic diversity is incredibly important. Race is usually associated with biology and linked with physical characteristics such as skin color or hair texture. Ethnicity is linked with cultural expression and identification. For example, someone's race might be white, but their ethnicity might be German or Dutch.

Both employers and employees have responsibilities when it comes to promoting a community of respect and inclusion of racial and ethnic diversity in the workplace. Employers should act as facilitators and purveyors of knowledge to improve relations among the employees. This includes continuously working on the development of diversity policy and implementation. Likewise, management and leaders in the business should be trained to ensure the improvement and promotion of awareness of racial discrimination and ethnic diversity in the workplace. Examples of discrimination include racist jokes, stereotyping, denial of promotions or certain roles, and segregating employees to certain jobs because of their race or ethnicity.

Also under the umbrella of discrimination are microaggressions. Microaggressions are the kinds of remarks, questions, or actions that are painful because they have to do with a person's race or ethnicity that is discriminated against or stereotyped. A key part of what makes microaggressions harmful and often difficult to identify is that they happen casually, frequently, and often without any harm intended. An example of a microaggression is an Asian-American employee being complimented for speaking perfect English, but it's actually his first language. Or perhaps a Black man notices that a white woman flinches and clutches her bag as she sees him in the elevator she is about to enter.

The responsibility of making new hires feel comfortable in a diverse and inclusive workplace is also up to the employees. Employees and organizations tasked with protecting workers' rights should lobby companies for strong ethnic diversity policies, ensuring all workers enjoy equal opportunities at all stages of the employment cycle, including access to employment training, promotion, and retirement. Employees also have an important role in raising awareness among themselves on the right to a workplace free from racial discrimination and in supporting coworkers when they issue complaints.

Preventing a Broken Onboarding Process

Making sure your employee has a positive orientation experience is crucial to preventing a broken onboarding process. A solid employee onboarding process is necessary to help your new hires settle down in their jobs, get to know the organization, obtain clarity in their job objectives, and forge a good relationship with other employees. If their experience fails to live up to expectations, then your new hire might regret their decision to accept the job offer. The negative impression left by a poor onboarding process might affect their perceptions, give them prejudiced notions about the organization, and ultimately cause them to quit early.

As part of the Strategic Advisor Board, Kara will help you develop a successful onboarding process to ensure new hires stay at your organization. The target audience and traffic are key to marketing and to business, but making sure your onboarding process is not broken is how you compete in this market. The Strategic Advisor Board will help you to create an environment of inclusion and respect, including an understanding of group development, as well as how to reduce your turnover rate. Once those steps are achieved, the SAB will guide you in engaging your potential clients and persuading them that you are the answer to all their problems.

The Strategic Advisor Board is here to help you navigate the multifaceted and complex challenges that obstruct you from scaling your business. Growing a business quickly requires special attention to customers' needs, wants, and desires. With Kara's extensive background in fixing a broken onboarding process, you will have the resources and support to focus on developing products and communication practices that will fill customer gaps and grow your company.

By employing the help of the Strategic Advisor Board and Kara's expertise, your business is guaranteed to expand its reach. By targeting the needs of certain markets and creating relationships with clients that continually add value, you can create a competitive advantage. Your new and improved form of brand cultivation will gain attention, making clients recognize and remember your business. In engaging the SAB's professional knowledge, you will surpass the superficial client relationships your competitors have, and you will build a deep, trusting, long-lasting relationship with your clients that will keep them coming back and referring you to their friends, family, and network connections. Your impact will increase exponentially from where it was before you enlisted the help of the Strategic Advisor Board.

5
ADAPTATION

About

Mike Jackson brings over thirty years of operational, consulting, and technical experience to the Strategic Advisor Board. Specializing in revenue cycle management, he has acquired a unique skill set that encompasses systems analysis and design, staff training and development, leadership management, and more. Mike's experience with the military and medical expertise situates him as an expert in business adaptation strategy. He consults with medical professionals to create reaction plans and adaptation strategies for a constantly changing environment. Mike helps medical professionals to achieve growth in their Wilderness and Austere Medical Training courses, focusing on special operations medicine, prehospital medicine, emergency medicine, and critical care medicine.

Mike strives to bring the human factor to businesses, helping them to experience growth through a deep understanding of their employees and their clients. He shows businesses how to share and impart their goals and vision with their employees, gaining them as an asset. Once employees are a better asset to business leaders, they will, in turn, be better advocates with clients.

Mike has more recently focused on strategic consulting services around provider relationships in the healthcare industry. His experience also includes developing and implementing policies and procedures, enforcing leadership standards, and assisting clients in implementing quality programs. Given his depth and breadth of expertise, he is also a regular facilitator and guest speaker at regional, national, and international healthcare conferences. Mike also consults for the Department of Defense, where he is the "go-to" advisor for all special operations training in the medical field and a senior advisor to the special operations community on all things medical.

Mike Jackson grew up in California in a military family. After high school, he joined the US Army and served his nation for the next 27 years as a Special Operations Medical Sergeant. His training was in environmental policy management and the medical industry.

System Resilience

Every business was challenged when the pandemic affected our daily practices and disrupted our revenue streams. Many businesses were forced to change what they offered customers and how they acquired their changing client base. People were spending less money, they were not able to conduct business face-to-face, and businesses were just completely closed. This effectively climinated a revenue stream for the business for a period of six weeks, and consumer behavior would take even longer to recover. In fact, we are still dealing with the recovery a year and a half later.

Small businesses can develop resilience to these outside economic forces by implementing ways of quick adaptation within their operations.

Flow of Communication

The single most important factor in maintaining your business infrastructure in times of growth, maintenance, or crisis is the communication network within your business. When businesses are confronted with a challenge, it is critical to make sure everyone within the business understands the details. As a CEO and manager, Mike can begin this collective problem-solving before a crisis hits. Giving agency and empowerment to everyone in the business leads to connection and dedication. The interdependence gained from the Strategic Advisor Board between employees will help a business get through any challenge that confronts the business.

Environmental Adaptation

As business owners, we continually think about effective and productive internal practices so we can have the most profitable business. We reflect upon successful methods and practices from the past to create systems that will be most effective in the future. We can develop successful systems, but when an outside crisis affects our revenue, how can we adapt? We need to be as prepared as we can for potential crises.

One strategy for adaption comes out of the recent pandemic. The businesses that have survived and succeeded through the challenges wrought by the pandemic should document their reactionary measures and procedures, which worked well. The documentation will prepare a business to handle the next crisis that emerges by providing a reflection. When a business reflects upon previous responses, they anticipate future challenges and prepare to adjust to variations emerging from the next crisis.

Our business needs to adjust to the outside environment to be able to survive and thrive. A business succeeds together with its external environment and potentially fails in conjunction with the environment. When we recognize the duality as a business owner, we will build out practices to adjust to any stimulus in the outside environment.

Reflection

It is critical for a business to assess practices and explore ideas that can make the business more cohesive. Businesses that invest in employee development can increase the productivity of their business by over twenty percent. That increased productivity translates to a rise in efficiency and profit. Invest in training, hire a business coach for an objective view of your business, or explore the practices of other business professionals to help improve the culture of your business.

Leaders are a crucial part of the business. They make a commitment to improving their professional skills, and the business will only benefit from the professional development. Ideas Mike and SAB might bring to your leadership include joining professional groups like the local chamber, business leader groups, a Toastmasters club, or even audit a class at a local college to help understand new local and national business trends. Not only will one grow as a leader for their business and employees, but they will also increase the visibility of their business.

Successful businesses follow a similar recipe: A healthy infrastructure; consistent communication with potential, current, and previous clients; and a strong business culture. Planning activities to support each of these areas on a regular basis will help prepare your business for the next stage of growth. Business growth is a challenge, but a strong business infrastructure with simple business habits can prepare your business for growth and profit.

Changing Consumer Behavior

Consumer behavior has changed in the past few months. While purchases are currently centered on the most basic needs, people are shopping more consciously, buying local, and are embracing digital commerce. To manage isolation, consumers are using digital means to connect, learn, and play—and they will continue to.

Consumers are responding to the crisis in a variety of ways. Some feel anxious and worried, fueling panic-buying of staples and hygiene products. At the other extreme, some consumers remain indifferent to the pandemic and are continuing their business as usual, despite recommendations from government and health professionals. Organizations will need to understand how their own consumers are reacting and develop customized and personalized marketing strategies for each target market

Consumers are flooded with information, are looking to make a connection in their business relationships, and be a part of a community. Here are some tips to successfully engage consumers in your own organization.

1) Engage your personality in your marketing

One of the biggest advantages of matching your personality to your job is the greater ease of connecting with your colleagues and clients. Consumers trust people much more than products or services. When a consumer knows about the person and brand behind the service, that increases the business opportunity. When planning your next piece of content, try to write like you talk, lose the cliches, use lighthearted visuals, and add videos!

2) Transparency within your business

Customer transparency is a business practice that values corporate honesty and encourages companies to communicate positive and negative information with their customers. Put plainly, it is a term that encompasses a value system meant to put the customer first, to present them with all of the necessary information so that they can make an educated purchase. Have a clear articulation of what the consumer can expect from a business transaction with you. You are the one that creates a comfortable and trusting atmosphere with your potential and future clients.

3) Discuss the results

What are the direct results of engaging in a business transaction with you and your business? What are the intangible results? When a client is connected to the larger core commitment of your business, referral and return service will increase. You will also engage a new type of customer—people begin to trust you when they know you are invested in creating a solution for them. If you do this, you'll create a strong foundation for your business.

Let's create a custom plan for growth in your small business to help you thrive despite the economic condition.

ADAPTATION

One of the most important lessons in the post-pandemic era of business is that businesses must be prepared to react to the outside economic environment. Develop strategies to create a process in your business that allows for quick reaction time. The systems in your business may be operating at full operational efficiency, but if they are not ready to adapt and change to the economy, it will be challenging to maintain your business.

6
COMMUNICATION

About

Just as the communication of a business's brand is essential to maintain a linear marketing strategy across platforms, effective customer communication is vital to decreasing turnover and increasing sales. Joel Phillips, Director and VP of Technology of Strategic Advisor Board (SAB), has decades of engineering profit turnaround for businesses, including his own, by dialing in on customer engagement, specifically in the form of digital interaction. His expertise in systems, automation, blockchain, and technology give him a unique upper hand in the information age of today. Phillips, beyond his heart as a driven corporate leader, is also highly experienced in working with start-ups, digital marketing, marketing software development, app development, data and analytics, and cybersecurity. His reach expands from the field of real estate to e-Commerce to the automotive industry. Phillips's deep knowledge of the business world and ever-changing approach to stay ahead of today's shifting consumer environment makes him a great asset to the Strategic Advisor Board and to businesses around the globe.

Joel Phillips has crafted his own personal brand from the ground up. His extensive professional experience in the field of technology, along with his MBA in technology management from the University of Phoenix, laid the groundwork for his own businesses: Proshark, Anthenem Blockchain, WhoTakesCoin, and J. Phillips, Inc./Lighthouse Properties, among others. A common thread that projected and continues to elevate Phillips to each advancement in his career is his laser focus on lowering operating expenses and increasing revenue. While this may seem like an obvious key to business success, it is often a massive, seemingly insurmountable hurdle for many companies. He is driven to innovate, define, test, measure and refine systems and processes to maximize efficiency and accuracy. Phillips understands there is not a one-size-fits-all path to growth, but he is an analyst at his core; his ability to apply past, proven solutions and integrate them with emerging technology to help businesses stay ahead of their competitors is unprecedented.

Customer Messaging and Digital Presence

Joel brings a new perspective to the "How to Increase Sales Fast" sort of question and Google search. There is, of course, validity to a cost-benefit analysis, a new investment, or a financial reorganization in a business's efforts to grow and scale to a new level; however, oftentimes, one vital variable is overlooked: the customer. Customer messaging and communication, from marketing and advertising to customer service to follow ups and surveys, maintain equal weight in customer acquisition and retention. Customer relations are no longer contingent on a business's employee's ability to provide great customer service in person. As the consumer market adapts to today's rapidly changing technology, so should your business's approach to customer communication.

Joel is certainly not a rookie in this field, and his expertise is vital to the service that SAB offers to businesses around the globe. As the CEO and founder of Proshark, a start-up focused on building relationships through digital interaction while protecting client and consumer data, he thrives in the intersection of new technological advances and old-school customer relations. Proshark combines multiple digital marketing channels into custom and semi-custom inbound and outbound solutions designed to improve a business's marketing budget efficiency. In line with SAB's core values and services, excessive financial investment or high-end consulting fees are not necessary to grow and scale. Joel leverages the online platform to provide data analytics, modeling, segmenting, and testing to improve customer engagement while also taking strategic steps to utilize security tools and defensive measures to protect your websites and data.

A high-quality, high-functioning website is essential to your business's online presence; it is your advertisement, business development, business card, showroom, sales department, fulfillment center, and customer acquisition and retention. Sales and marketing automation is one of many customized services that Joel uses to propel your business to a new dimension of customer communication and messaging. Consumers, becoming increasingly more remote in nature, determines how they want to communicate with the companies they do business with. It is crucial for your business to stay up to date in customer messaging if you desire to maintain the longevity of their success in their field, which you do because you're reading this book. Chat boxes, texting, email, etc., are quickly replacing face-to-face interaction. No longer are first impressions experienced in a brick-and-mortar store, but rather through your company's website in your customer's computer, tablet, or smartphone. Before your business has the chance to prove its credibility and differentiate your service from your competitors, you must first secure the interest of your customer through effective marketing and customer messaging.

Likewise, optimization and ranking hold just as much weight as social media campaigns, landing pages, and other digital marketing content. Search engine optimization (SEO) is only one opportunity for your business to grow its digital presence when working with SAB. Video SEO (VSEO) and keywords research and ranking generate traction—never again will your marketing campaign go unseen. Marketing of any kind that does not yield profit is simply a waste of time and money, something you cannot afford if you want to win in business. Effective marketing and websites lead to customer interest and communication, customer communication (if taken advantage of, which you should) turns to profit, and profit results in growth and scale. All of the above are possible and actually enjoyable with SAB (we know something you may not be able to say about the business consulting firm you have worked with in the past).

Consistent Customer Engagement and Innovation

Work, in all senses of the word, is becoming more and more technological, with the internet being the most accessible and widely used platform. SAB capitalizes on the opportunity to use websites as a source of not just survival but revenue. Joel, along with the collective SAB team, walks you through each detail of your business, which inevitably includes your website. Beginning with website development and security to create an effective online presence, to digital marketing to generate traffic, to enhancing automation to free up time and gather valuable customer trends and needs, to creating apps and other software to expand reach; SAB will help you identify and determine what your business needs (and wants) and gets you there, quickly.

Results matter, and those results, especially surrounding customer communication, are impacted by the consistency of your business's customer engagement across all points of contact, your website being only one of many. Other points of contact can be physical (in-person conversation, phone calls, traditional print copy, etc.), digital (webchat, video messaging, email campaigns, etc.), and social (social media, text messaging, podcasts, etc.). Each platform provides you a unique opportunity to engage your customers in a relatively inexpensive, convenient, and quick way, but each will remain dormant without the proper tools and communication strategy, an opportunity that SAB is passionate about optimizing.

Take social media, for instance. Social media posts are only one aspect of this ever-growing, ever-changing platform. You need to effectively communicate your business, service, products, etc., but you also must take advantage of the opportunity to use customer accounts to have one-on-one communication with your customers via direct/instant messaging. Hashtags and account tags provide the opportunity for increased customer reviews and exposure to your business. Comments and complaints can be quickly resolved and, if handled publicly, generate credibility for your business by showing other customers what kind of high-quality customer service you provide. Live videos, popular songs and dances, stories, and highlights all make information and company culture readily accessible and marketable to a wide range of consumers worldwide. Social media allows your business to be more responsive than ever and maintain a regular, real-time connection to your customers. Doing so can take your business from one of many to an integral part of your customers' lives (and their friends' lives too).

In order to make the most of each point of contact, customer engagement must be consistent across platforms in order to reap the most significant results. When your customer visits your website, for example, the same messaging, product availability, hours of operation, etc., should be displayed as your Facebook account. If you respond to emails in 24 hours, you need to be responding in a similar manner to those who direct messages to you on Instagram. If a charitable donation is a critical marketing message to your brand, your customer needs to experience the same emphasis during their in-store visit. The possibilities for customer communication and engagement via each of these various platforms are endless and, nevertheless, overwhelming. SAB, and the tools and expertise that they employ, is capable of enhancing each channel of a business's customer engagement in order to guarantee they are making the most of each point of contact (Chatbox automation, communication skills training for your employees, task delegating—the list goes on).

Excelling in consistent customer engagement is inherent to unifying your customers' experience. The familiar "Seven Times Factor" states that a customer must be exposed to an ad seven times before they buy it. If five of those seven times their experience is different, the likelihood of your marketing efforts resulting in a sale consequently diminishes. Trusting SAB to streamline your channels of customer engagement will undoubtedly result in an increase in profit, which ultimately frees up your precious time, space, and resources so you can focus on what matters most.

Know Your Customer, Better Your Product, Increase Your Sales

Social media, as a continued example, is also a great tool to collect information about your customers, trends, and business partnerships. Social media accounts portray a great deal of information about your customers' lifestyles and provide you with a unique insight into their changing needs and wants. Social media, given its collective nature, highlights customer trends and the way seasons, fads, and styles are accepted by your particular target market. In the same light, customer accounts and other information gathered by effective customer communication can also be a great source for new ideas. By taking advantage of the information gathered across various points of customer connections, the more likely your business is to successfully serve your market, provide unique services different from your competitors, and increase your sales.

Every business strategy must stay flexible and adapt to changes to the market, the customer, and the technology in order to yield the most profit. Changes in your company, in services, or perhaps location are one of the many reasons to maintain regular contact with your customers. Take Blockchain and cryptocurrency, for instance. There is a change in current quickly arising, and the whole market will experience a paradigm shift. Cryptocurrency is a payment system of coins based on the Blockchain. SAB, thanks to the expertise offered by Phillips, is prepared to help your business take advantage of this unexplored payment system. Communicating this new change in your business operations to your customers will be critical to reaping the most return due to the fact that many of your clients will fail to appreciate the value it offers them until they're told. So do it; tell them.

Keeping your customers informed is necessary for a business's survival but asking your customers questions is necessary to achieve growth. You need to understand what your customers care about, what faults they see in certain products and services you offer, etc. Asking questions and listening to your customers' needs gives you the upper hand in tailoring each part of your business as a solution to their problem and takes the guesswork out of development. Many businesses miss this great opportunity (do not be one of those businesses). Failing to ask your target market if a product or service you offer is beneficial or not limits growth. Your business's time and resources should only be spent on maximizing the products, services, and approach that yields the most return. Growth cannot afford inefficiency (hint: neither can you). Trying to force sales of services that provide little to no benefit or solution for your customers will always end in disappointment for both you and your customer.

Giving your customers what they want builds your company's credibility. If your business's focus is on forcing a sale, you run the risk of possibly angering a customer in the attempt and can quickly destroy the likelihood of that customer buying in the future. Even worse, it would increase the chances that that same customer gives your business a poor review, either online or via word of mouth. The main goal of all customer engagement must remain serving your customers. SAB exists to help you, in every field, achieve and maintain genuine, wholesome results that maintain your credibility, all while boosting your bottom line.

Connection Generates Trust, Trust Generates Sales

Building credibility will build trust, and trust will ultimately increase sales (something SAB's team of experts know all too well). Effective, consistent, regular communication with your customers increases your business's chances of overcoming challenges. Consider a market crash or global pandemic, for instance. Customers will always be more inclined to purchase from the companies they trust, especially in a circumstance where their resources are limited due to market changes. When your company has a customer base that feels connected; feels a sense of loyalty from your business that truly cares about their needs and not just the dollar they provide you, your business will likely maintain projected revenue goals and even grow, while other businesses who have not built up this customer base may experience hardship; some even forced to close their doors.

SAB is equipped to teach you how to effectively navigate crisis management in a way that capitalizes on the opportunity to serve your customers where they are at. Even in times of distress, there are always new ways to grow and scale your business. However, without the foundation of trust, your efforts to grow and scale will remain an unreachable goal. You'll never be able to make a lucrative change (take implementing cryptocurrency into your business, for instance) if your customers are hesitant to do business with you. Like a savings account, it is simply not wise for you to not invest in knowing, understanding, and serving your customers. On a rainy day, the businesses that have genuine, credible assets built from their relationships can look to their customers to help float them to shore. If you want to survive, do the same; connect with your customer, do it well, and do it regularly.

Those very customer relationships that lead to survival and growth are the result of the quality of customer service your business provides. The foundation of great customer service is built on communication between your business and your customer. Effective communication is undoubtedly the connecting variable between your company's product or service and turning it into profit, but that sales pitch does not inherently cultivate a lifetime customer. Connection and emotion generate more loyalty than simply communicating concrete information. Again, knowing the target market you serve is paramount in bringing about return buyers. You must provide value to your customers. If every effort to connect with your customers ends in an ask for a sale, your customer will be quickly burnt out. No one likes to feel used, and customers are not exempt. In order to generate sales exponentially, your customer must feel like your business exists to serve them.

This type of value—the kind that creates the type of connections that generates profit—needs to exist in addition to the product or service that you're selling. In other words, the product or service that generates revenue has to offer value in order to catch your customer's attention, but relational value should be generated separately from your source of revenue. Oftentimes that value, from the customer's perspective, is offered at zero cost to them.

For example, consider a real estate agent who desires to generate sales. They should be asking their customers specific questions to identify their needs outside of the property they are interested in buying that will, of course, result in a profit for the agent. Suppose this real estate agent, after getting to know their current customer, has identified their client's desire to build new streams of income to meet some of their financial goals. In addition to providing the client with the necessary information and tools to connect them to the property that meets their housing needs and financial goals (perhaps a multi-family property that could be partial rental property), the agent may also connect the client to a preferred business consulting firm in order for them to grow their other business ventures and increase those streams of income to see results, fast.

By providing this seemingly "free" resource to the client, the agent is providing value that extends beyond the marketed service as a real estate agent. By doing so, the agent understands what the client truly wants, cultivates relational connection with the client and strengthens advantageous business connections with the referral, and ultimately generates more sales because those clients will be more motivated to return to this agent when they look to buy another property, and more likely to spread a positive review via word of mouth. This domino effect occurs because the client has a relational foundation built on that truth that the agent cares for the whole being of their clients, rather than just the revenue that they can provide them.

Free resources can generate value by reinforcing a business's character and integrity. Character and integrity ultimately generate credibility. A customer is more likely to purchase from a business that has been serving them or providing a need or solution for them before they ever entered their credit card information.

For instance, a brick-and-mortar store could capitalize on an opportunity to serve their clients by advertising the season's new launch in an email campaign while also including information in that email that is a free resource and of value to their known customer. Consider, if a bike shop has a new mountain bike for sale, they may include information for a free class that they are hosting to teach their members and customers how to repair the bikes that they currently own. This free resource not only sends a message to their current customers that they care about keeping them happy, but it also helps them acquire new customers by marketing their new product and the holistic customer service that they will provide even after they have secured the sale. This is a true connection. This is business done well. This is what SAB understands is necessary for you to grow and scale your business.

On the contrary, poor communication has the potential to turn your customers away, and existing customers may lose trust and faith in your business and seek the same products and services elsewhere. It is crucial to identify all areas of communication that cause sales to decline and make changes immediately. This is especially common in businesses that have a large number of employees or where there is a large gap between decision-making leaders and the employees that are directly serving customers and, thus, being the voice of that business. Communication skills training is one way to guarantee that all channels and streams of communication are linear throughout your team.

Providing customers with great customer service is not an instinctive trait. It is a learned skill. You must invest in teaching your employees how to communicate to your customers in a way that aligns with your business strategy (if you desire to see results quickly, that is). SAB knows how to integrate both personal, digital, technological, and other forms of communication and engagement in order to make sure that every point of contact that your customer has with your business is consistent and effective.

Identifying the areas where you need to grow can be daunting. SAB realizes that if you do not know what to fix, the idea of trying to find a solution to an unidentified problem will seem impossible. In the same way, the thought of innovation can be daunting. Times are constantly changing, and vehicles of communication are continually evolving. SAB takes the mystery out of how to stay ahead of your competitors. No longer will you have to waste your valuable time, money, or energy trying to crack the mystery of improving your business. By improving your communication with your customers in every channel, you can experience a real increase in sales. Yet, just as someone in the driver's seat of a car is unlikely to identify a blind spot because they are inside the vehicle, you may struggle to identify areas where you need to grow. However, someone who is looking from the outside is more likely to identify the blind spot that the driver was unable to see, given their different perspectives. In the same way, SAB is able to partner with you to identify the areas in your business that could use improvement to take you to the next level.

7
FULFILLMENT

About

Joe Trujillo is a competent and performance-driven professional with exceptional procedural skills and a passion for resolving complex problems through innovative solutions. With proven leadership abilities in managing diverse workgroups, Joe has over 20 years of combined career experience in operations, communications, manufacturing, quality control, auditing, and workforce training. Joe has a high-level aptitude in business administration, process implementation, and project management.

Through the various managerial roles in his career, Joe also possesses a strong familiarity with government and corporate organizational structures. Trained in LEAN/6S methodology, Joe employs strategic thinking for both the individual and collaborative environments. Joe has proficiency in performing needs assessments, examining procedures/processes, and gathering appropriate data to measure efficiency.

As a U.S. military veteran, Joe understands the importance of core values and completing "the mission" to succeed. Joe takes pride in coaching industry leaders on the ideologies of working numerous duties related to management while ensuring proper dissemination of company productivity.

Joe holds a master's degree in adult education from Kansas State University and a bachelor's degree in workforce education and development from Southern Illinois University. Joe's greatest passion is teaching and learning, as well as being able to facilitate a group of professionals and contribute to the mentorship of junior personnel. A native of Texas, Joe lives in Arkansas with his wife and three children.

Joe's extensive experience has culminated in his expertise in his own personal brand: customer fulfillment. Customer fulfillment refers to business strategies used to get products and services to consumers. It comes down to choosing a strategy and implementing it thoughtfully. Having a well-outlined and smooth order fulfillment process will help your business continue to draw customers and satisfy them with your products. Working with Joe and the Strategic Advisor Board will result in increased first-pass yields, higher production throughput, process improvements, project/program implementation, lowered costs, and increased revenues.

Division of Labor

An important component of customer fulfillment is the division of labor. This refers to the assignment of different parts of a manufacturing process to different people in order to improve efficiency. It is essential to economic progress because it allows people to specialize in particular tasks. This specialization makes workers more productive, which reduces the total cost of producing goods or providing a service. A basic example of this strategy is Ford's motor factories. With the assembly line, each worker had a specific job to do. If a worker only installs the transmission, they will be very good at that one job. However, if a worker installs everything in the car, then they will be just okay at every job and will be more likely to make mistakes, costing the business money and resulting in unhappy customers.

There are many benefits to implementing a division of labor in your workplace. Workers need less training as they only have to master a small number of tasks. It is quicker to use one particular tool and do one job. No time is wasted with a worker dropping a tool and then picking up another. Workers can gain loyalty and a sense of achievement from their branch of production. There is no need to move around the workplace because the half-finished goods come to them. Workers can also concentrate on those jobs which best suit their skills and personality.

Applying a division of labor in your workplace will aid in your customer fulfillment. Each department can focus on its specific job, which is giving your customers the best experience possible, rather than being spread thin by multiple jobs and responsibilities. Not only will it help scale your business, but it will make your customers happy and more likely to return to your business, as well as leave a good review and refer others. By having better quality products, a better fulfillment process, and fewer mistakes because of your division of labor, your customers will keep coming back to your business.

Division of labor goes hand in hand with the chain of command. The chain of command describes the way in which organizations traditionally structure their reporting relationships. Reporting relationships refers to an organizational structure in which every employee is placed somewhere on an organizational chart. Employees report to those who are listed above them on the organizational chart.

For example, at the top of the organizational chart is the CEO of a business. The vice presidents are under the CEO, so they report to the CEO. Under the vice presidents are the directors/managers, and under the directors/managers are roles like product engineer, product specialist, graphic designer, web developer, etc.

When every employee reports to one other employee, decisions and communication are tightly controlled, and they flow down the chain of command throughout the organization. This is an intentional, traditional structure for the chain of command in organizations that want to tightly control the dissemination of information and the allocation of power and control. Historically, this is the preferred structure for an organization. Moreover, this allows each person to have a specific role, where they can focus on their specific responsibilities.

A clearly communicated and maintained chain of command can improve company morale, promote better teamwork, and enhance manager-employee relationships. Front-line employees who go directly to managers with questions and concerns create a closer relationship at the team or department level. For this reason, the customers will benefit from your chain of command.

Once you have achieved a successful division of labor and chain of command, your business is prepared to implement a fulfillment strategy. Because of the requirements of fulfillment strategies, each department has to be comfortable with their responsibilities, as well as prepared to communicate with higher-ups if any problems arise.

Creating a Fulfillment Strategy

Whether you choose to keep your fulfillment strategy in-house or outsource it, setting up or updating a fulfillment strategy is a delicate process. You cannot shut down the business while you switch gears, so the transition needs to be smooth and as quick as possible. The best way to ensure success is to plan carefully.

There are two kinds of fulfillment strategies: customer relationship management software and third-party logistics companies.

First, choose a strategy. Which system is going to work the best for you and your team members now, and which system will scale the easiest in the future as your company grows? Decide, specifically, what services can be done in-house and what services will need to be outsourced. Walk through the fulfillment process (Receiving, Inventory Storage, Picking, Packing, Shipping, and Returns Processing) and make sure each step is covered. Having a division of labor is especially important for this step.

Second, set up your system. Whether it's software or business partnerships, it needs to be in place, and your team members need to be comfortable with it before it starts affecting the business. Are the current team members sufficiently trained to set up your system, or do you need to temporarily hire contractors to get a new system installed?

Third, select and set up key performance indicators. Typically, the top five key performance indicators are revenue per client, average class attendance, client retention rate, profit margin, and average daily attendance. Be prepared to measure success from the start. Which metrics you choose to focus on will depend on what problems you are trying to solve. In addition to this hard data, consider implementing customer satisfaction surveys to see how customer needs are being met with the new strategy compared to before.

Finally, start small with your new fulfillment strategy. Roll out the new strategy with one product line and carefully track the progress. Work out the kinks and make sure your customers are happy before moving over to another process in the fulfillment strategy.

As previously mentioned, there are two types of fulfillment strategies: customer relationship management software and third-party logistics companies. You and your team members need to decide how much fulfillment you are capable of handling in-house and how much you want to outsource. You can also use a combination of the two fulfillment strategies. It all comes down to your business's resources.

CRM Technology

Customer Relationship Management (CRM) software is a tracking system used to organize customer data. CRM technology lets you store customer and prospective contact information, identify sales opportunities, record service issues, and manage marketing campaigns, all in one central location. It also makes information about every customer interaction available to anyone at your company who might need it.

CRM technology is commonly used in sales and marketing to streamline and personalize communications, but it also eases the customer fulfillment process by processing orders, storing shipping and tracking information, creating and managing transaction documents, tracking inventory, and running reports.

This technology is a great option for businesses who want to keep a close eye on a scaling business or product line. Most systems integrate well with the existing software, and it offers benefits to sales and marketing teams. It is also a great option if you and your business want to keep everything in-house. However, remember that this software can only do so much. The product still has to get sorted, packaged, and shipped. As your company grows, the more you and your business will most likely need a third-party logistics company.

3PL Company

Third-party logistics (3PL) companies offer solutions in warehousing, packaging, assembly, and distribution under one roof, so you can leave some, or all, of the order fulfillment to supply chain experts. UPS, or the United Parcel Service, is a great example of a 3PL company.

A 3PL company can provide a range of services, such as setup, shipping, and customer service. Most can manage inventory, optimize transit time, process returns and claims, and provide the data you need on your unique key performance indicators. You do not need to invest in warehouse space or extended technology, and you do not need to hire and train more internal employees.

When choosing a 3PL company, several factors need to be taken into consideration. How big is the warehouse? Where is the warehouse located in proximity to airports, ports, and railways? What is the 3PL company's reputation with other customers they have served? Do they maintain OSHA requirements? What is their flexibility for overtime during peak seasons? Most importantly, how good are they at communicating?

While there are many benefits, outsourcing to a 3PL company might not be cost-effective for your business. Local companies that handle their own distribution with ease might not benefit from outsourcing. However, if your business is struggling, reaching out to a 3PL company might be the answer for you.

While production and distribution are obviously the largest components when it comes to customer fulfillment, a smaller and more underrated variable that carries significant weight in the process may surprise you.

CUSTOMER SERVICE

One of the most important parts of customer fulfillment is customer service. A mismanaged order fulfillment process can be problematic and result in an angry customer, a bad review, and a poor reputation. Let's face it: no matter how efficient and smooth a fulfillment strategy is, mistakes happen. A customer order can be postponed, damaged, or go missing. As a responsible business, make the existing fulfillment process smooth so that the maximum number of customers are retained. Knowing how to communicate with your customers will ensure that you minimize the risk of losing customers.

The main parts of customer service are rapport and active listening. You and your team members need to participate in these activities in order for your customers to feel comfortable enough to share their thoughts and feelings, as well as for them to continue coming back to your business. You will better understand your customers' wants and needs, and your business will have a better retention rate overall.

Rapport is a harmonious relationship between two or more people in which both people understand each other's feelings or ideas and communicate well. Rapport is a process that does not just happen; it must be built day-by-day and is a dynamic, fluctuating affair. To build rapport with a customer means to start a relationship where the team worker and the customer understand each other's personalities.

You and your team members can build rapport by asking questions about your customers' backgrounds and by actively listening, an undertaking that is beneficial to both you and the customer. Active listening requires the listener to fully concentrate, understand, respond, and then remember what is being said. Active listening can be shown by asking questions to clarify, maintaining eye contact, showing interest, withholding judgment, and paying attention to what is being said rather than thinking about what can be said in response. By doing this, the team member shows respect toward the customer and allows the customer to feel more comfortable, which can result in a sale due to the customer's increasing receptivity.

Sensing active listening in social interactions is accompanied by an improvement in the recollected impressions of relevant experiences and is thought to arouse positive feelings. This means that if a team member demonstrates active listening, the customer will leave the conversation with positive feelings that can motivate them to buy something, leave a good review, refer family or friends, and come back to your business.

Moreover, trust builds rapport. Your customers will learn to trust you and your team members if you do what you say. Keep your commitments, call when you say you will, and always follow through. Be careful not to make promises you might not be able to keep. Too many people make well-intentioned commitments, only to find themselves unable to find time to fulfill them. They may not always lose a sale because of this, but they are certainly not building the kind of trust that will make a customer happy to give referrals.

Another way to build trust is to demonstrate that you are interested in their well-being beyond your own profit potential. This is very similar to active listening, but it goes further into action. Know and appreciate your customers' needs beyond your product. See what you can do to help them meet those needs. Little things like finding information for them or putting them in touch with other suppliers tend to make a big difference.

Sometimes, customers are just angry and need to vent freely. It is difficult to build rapport with an angry customer, so let them get it all out first. Even if you have the solution to their problem, it is best not to cut them off in between. If you interrupt, the customer will only get more irritated, thinking you do not care about them. Once the customer is done speaking, show empathy to indicate that you have understood their situation, and then provide solutions to the customer. Additionally, use the right words and phrases when dealing with an angry customer.

Here are some phrases best suited to dealing with angry customers. If a customer does not have a legitimate grievance and instead is just offloading their frustration, respond with

"I'm sorry that you feel this way," "What I'll do right now is…" or "We really do appreciate this feedback." If a customer has a legitimate grievance, respond with "Thank you so much for letting us know about this," "I'm so sorry to hear about this," "Thank you so much for your patience/understanding," or "I will do (this action) for you right away."

Finally, every single person will have to deal with the abusive customer, who will just hurl insults and threats because they can. Even more important than verbal language is the ability to stay cool under pressure and strive to restore calm. Some phrases you can use are "I truly understand your concern, but unfortunately, we cannot tolerate the kind of language you are using right now," "I'm sorry you're so upset right now. Would you like for us to call you back when you feel a little calmer?" or "I apologize, but if you continue this use of language, I will be forced to end this call."

Customer Fulfillment is Key

More and more, fulfillment is what drives the loyalty that keeps people coming back to your business rather than to your competitors. A good or bad fulfillment process will impact your business. To grow, you need to keep the promises you make and deliver orders profitably.

Customer fulfillment is the backbone of company success, but there is no one-size-fits-all strategy. What works best for your brand might be a completely unique combination of team members and business partners, but if you are unsure, you can always explain your situation to Joe. Start by walking through your fulfillment process, honestly evaluating your needs, and putting together the plan that works best for your business and your customers.

As part of the Strategic Advisor Board, Joe helps you develop a successful customer fulfillment strategy for your business transactions. Marketing and products are important to your business's overall success, but a well-outlined and smooth customer fulfillment strategy is how you compete in this market. The Strategic Advisor Board will help you to understand your business's unique strategy, including whether to outsource or stay in-house, as well as how to implement that strategy. Once those steps are achieved, the SAB will guide you in retaining your current clients and persuading them that you are the answer to all their problems.

The Strategic Advisor Board is here to help you navigate the multifaceted and complex challenges that obstruct you from scaling your business. Growing a business quickly requires special attention to customers' needs, wants, and desires. With Joe's extensive background in developing an efficient customer fulfillment strategy, you'll have the resources and support to focus on developing products and communication practices that will fill customer gaps and grow your company.

By employing the help of the Strategic Advisor Board and Joe's expertise, your business is guaranteed to expand its reach. By targeting the needs of certain markets and creating relationships with clients that continually add value, you can create a competitive advantage. Your new and improved form of brand cultivation will gain attention, making clients recognize and remember your business. In engaging the SAB's professional knowledge, you will surpass the superficial client relationships your competitors have, and you will build a deep, trusting, long-lasting relationship with your clients that will keep them coming back and referring you to their friends, family, and network connections. Your impact will increase exponentially from where it was before you enlisted the help of the Strategic Advisor Board.

8
RELATIONSHIPS

About

Mike Owens is a seasoned business owner and operator with an extensive passion for helping other business owners and CEOs succeed. He has a specialty in helping businesses create a passive system of income, as well as guiding entrepreneurs through the rough waters of growing and scaling their companies in sequence. Focusing on smart business growth in a constantly changing economy, he is always highly focused on the customer and helping clients execute their strategies as quickly as possible.

Mike's professional background includes being a general manager to two international restaurant chains, owning and operating five restaurants that he created himself, and dedicating twenty years to a business consulting and coaching firm.

In one location, he was brought on to secure client contracts, union contracts, and revive profitability while stimulating growth in an ailing sector. At the time of taking on responsibility, this location had ten units and collectively lost one million dollars annually. Within 36 months, Mike and his team were operating in the positive, which was achieved using economies as a scale by opening more locations on second and third shifts and pivoting the business model to be more sustainable while utilizing new technology, product development, and reshaping the landscape. Operating efficiencies had to take on a new life in order to forecast anomalies that the market may bring. Prior to the pandemic, the model was fully implemented and, during the COVID-19 shutdown, Mike and his team remained solvent and continued to make results, despite the country's economic downturn.

No matter what the industry is, understanding the complexities of business helped prepare Mike with problem-solving skills while improving the efficiency of protocol and procedures. In addition, having the vision of knowing how and why to guide leadership through stages of growth and market pivots makes him an expert in his field. Growing a business fast requires special attention and focus on the clients' needs, wants, and desires. This means focusing on the problems to be solved that allow a business owner to offer a product that fills a gap in the marketplace quickly. Doing this means higher profits in the business and higher rates of customer acquisition and customer retainability. The faster a business can develop products that fill consumer gaps, the more your company will grow. This requires fast action in a rapid production mode to get ahead of the competition.

Mike, along with his wife Carrie and three children, live in Flint Hills, Kansas. Mike and his wife enjoy traveling, golf, CrossFit, and spending time with their grandchildren. They also are both involved in Freedom Hooves Therapeutic Riding Center, an organization dedicated to serving children and adults with disabilities through equine-assisted therapies. An alumnus of Johnson County Community College for

Hospitality and Business, his education inspired him to have a successful corporate career.

Developing quick and successful results for his clients is what Mike prides himself in. He helps clients to build a business model and implement the tools, plans, and support structures to drive their business to its optimal potential. With his assistance, businesses will be able to focus on each phase of growth to include short-term, mid-term, and long-term goals. These are the steps that will drive a business through a layered level of success, allowing a company to reinvest quickly and grow faster. Mike will help clients create fresh ideas, new concepts, and how to further those ideas with staff to earn winning products for the business as a whole.

What is a Referral Agent?

A referral agent is a person who makes money by referring customers or clients to a business or individual who can meet their needs. This term is commonly used in real estate. For example, a real estate referral agent is a real estate agent who refers a client to another real estate agent, who will then manage the client's real estate transaction. Real estate referral agents receive a portion of the commission on the real estate transaction a client conducts after they have been referred. Conversely, a business referral is when someone in your network recommends your business to a new prospect. This may happen spontaneously during organic conversation or as a result of conscious referral marketing efforts. This person may or may not earn money from referring you and your business.

If you provide a great customer experience, word-of-mouth referrals are bound to happen naturally, at no cost to you. However, a conscious effort to cultivate customer relationships will result in a higher ROI (return on investment) from your network. By purposefully building rapport with your customers, not only are you broadening your sphere of influence by tapping into your potential referrers' social circles, but referral prospects will be more open to working with your business since they know and trust the referrer. In addition, the referrer is providing a vote of confidence by making the recommendation, which is a powerful piece of social credibility.

Referral marketing has three main steps. First, identify key individuals in your sphere of influence, that being existing customers, business contacts, friends, family, and the like. Second, cultivate and invest in those relationships, completing favors and helping these key individuals whenever you can. Third, ask these people if they can refer others to your business. If you are especially talented at the first two steps, the third step might not even have to happen! This is easier said than done, so it is beneficial to implement referral marketing strategies and tactics as you move forward. Let's talk about some of those strategies to get referrals from customers.

First and foremost, the best strategy possible is to exceed expectations. Word of mouth is one of the single most powerful ways to gain referrals. However, it is mostly dependent on loyalty, which means it is something you have to earn. If you want to get your current or potential customers talking about your service, you have to captivate them. Go above and beyond for your customers not just by meeting their expectations but by sharing their content on social media, citing them in your blog content, and proving to be a resource for them. Then, the case will be made for you why they should tell their network about the great work you do.

If you want your customers to make referrals, give them a reason to talk about your company. As you approach your day-to-day business activities, you must constantly be innovating in the area of customer experience. Not only do you want to please them, but you want to charm them in a way that will put your business at the forefront of their minds. Stories are powerful, and if your customers are compelled to share their experiences, prospective clients will listen.

To create customer experiences that are noteworthy, understand where the customer is coming from. Ask yourself questions like, "What is their problem that I can solve? What does success look like to them?" Find a key area that will bridge that gap. Cross-reference those areas with the solutions that you provide and the solutions they are investing in. Understand that these are the things that they expect. Where you need to go above and beyond is with the things that will fill the gap but are out of scope or expectation. Finally? Deliver. It is possible that the answer lies in a new method of delivery, going above and beyond on a specific task, providing more value than you promised, or imagining new ways that the process can be more enjoyable.

The previous tips focus on charming the customer. Therefore, it stands to reason that you should keep existing customers engaged. Continually provide high points throughout the customer experience, as well as afterwards if you provide one-time services or purchases. Regularly invest in each of the customer relationships you make in your business, providing ways to keep them engaged with you so that you can remain at the forefront of their mind. This can be done by staying in touch post-sale and nurturing the relationship into a long-term connection, checking in to see how your product or service is helping the customer, continuing to provide value through avenues such as additional offerings, informative content, or semi-frequent check-ins, and providing an ongoing community or sharing a set of values.

Aligning with your customers' values is an important detail when engaging with current customers and bringing in prospective customers. Do your research to learn about what your customers truly value before asking them for a referral. Then, you can position your incentive or acknowledgment with those values, and you will be able to give them an idea of the impact they will have with a referral. For example, if your customers use your product for nonprofit fundraising, or if you know they are personally or professionally invested in advocacy for a cause, you could reward them for referrals with a donation in their name. Simple gestures like this can go a long way toward proving to customers that your relationship is a partnership, not just a business transaction.

If you are asking a customer to refer people to your business, they may expect the same from you. By offering to refer your customers to other companies, you will bring valuable bargaining chips to the negotiation table. Your customers will feel like they are getting equal compensation for the information they give up. However, be careful. Your relationship with your current customers is at stake whenever you refer them elsewhere. Make sure you're sending them to a company as great as yours, or they may end up blaming you for any misfortune.

When in doubt, offer incentives. Nobody likes to work for free, right? If you want to sweeten the deal and make sure your customers actually carefully search their networks for a good referral, offer them something valuable in return. Whether it is a gift certificate, a discount code, or a free month's subscription, give something back to your customers for connecting you with warm leads.

The best referrals come after the customer has had an opportunity to experience the value that you are capable of delivering. You would not ask your boss for a raise right after you missed the mark on your monthly quota, which is why it would not be appropriate to request a referral when you're under-delivering on what you promised a customer. To set yourself up for success, you have to prove yourself as referral-worthy. To ensure you are meeting (and exceeding) the needs and expectations of your existing customers, it is important that you're regularly collecting and acting on their feedback.

Feedback Loops

A feedback loop is the part of a system in which some portion (or all) of the system's output is used as input for future operations. What does that mean? Let's say you release a product. Customers love part A of the product, but they don't like part B of the product. Knowing that result, in your next product release, you will make sure to include lots of part A, but not any part B, right? That is the feedback loop.

Each feedback loop has a minimum of four stages. During the first stage, input is created. During the second stage, input is captured and stored. During the third stage, input is analyzed, and during the fourth stage, the insight gained from the analysis is used to make decisions.

Feedback loops can be either negative or positive. Negative feedback loops are self-regulating and useful for maintaining an optimal state within specific boundaries. An old-fashioned house thermostat that uses bang-bang control to turn a furnace on or off is a classic example of a self-regulating negative feedback loop. When the temperature drops to a predetermined low set point, the thermostat switches the heating system on. When the temperature reaches a predetermined high set point, the thermostat switches the heating system off.

Negative feedback loops are known for being stable but not especially accurate. For example, in the case of a home thermostat, there can be a fairly wide range of acceptable temperatures that can cause the heating system to have a fairly long response time. You have been in this situation; some people like their house to be cold, but some people like their house to be hot.

In contrast, positive feedback loops simply repeat actions that have been effective in the past. The intention of a positive feedback loop is to amplify a desired variable and naturally move the system away from its starting state to a desired state.

Problems can occur, however, when the positive feedback loop grows exponentially without any checks or balances. In such a scenario, a runaway positive feedback loop can make a system become unstable.

Let's talk about this in business terms. A negative feedback loop is a process where a company listens to customers' complaints or grievances and then uses that feedback to improve their products or customer service. It is considered a loop because the customers' feedback (output) is used as constructive input on a redesign of their product, creating a circle. The negative feedback loop benefits both businesses and customers—customers feel valued and respected by the business and are more likely to become long-term advocates for the brand, and the business's design is improved to increase customer satisfaction.

A positive feedback loop is a process where a company listens to employees' complaints or grievances and uses that feedback to improve internal structure and workplace satisfaction. As a result of improved workplace satisfaction, the company is then able to increase its profits. It is considered a loop because employees' feedback (output) is used as input on a restructuring of the work culture, creating a circle. A positive feedback loop can be a formal or informal process in which you collect employee feedback on their overall work satisfaction and respond to that feedback to make your employees happier.

While both feedback loops should absolutely be utilized within your company, a negative feedback loop will be the most beneficial to turning customers into referral agents. The first step in a negative feedback loop is receiving criticism. There are many ways you can gather negative feedback, such as customer surveys, social media or other online reviews, a comment box, complaint calls/emails, and reports from the customer service desk in your office. To be able to use the negative feedback in a positive manner, consider implementing a system to clearly record and categorize all complaints and concerns, as well as a time when you regularly review them, such as once per month.

To use the negative feedback well, you may need to follow up on complaints and concerns to understand what the issues are or what is causing them. Questions to ask could be, "What could we have done to improve your experience?" or "How would you change this product?" After you have collected and researched the negative feedback, you should analyze it thoroughly. A careful review can help you determine whether problems were one-time issues, serious product flaws, customer service failures, minor concerns, or some other reason. Categorizing complaints by their underlying issue will help you with the next step.

Determine how you can use the negative feedback to improve your process, product, service, or workplace. Implementing positive solutions based on negative feedback is what creates the loop. The purpose of using a negative feedback loop is to focus on constant improvement. Decide what actions you can take to respond to the criticism and create short- or long-term plans to enact those changes.

Finally, make sure your customers and employees understand your recent changes and the reason for those changes. You could put up a sign in your office, send out a press release, post on social media, send out an email, or add an explanation on product packaging. Notification is important because explaining the steps you are taking to improve may encourage customers to buy your product again, inspire loyalty, and of course, refer you to others. Ultimately, there is nothing better for your business than happy customers and happy employees, and the negative feedback loop is critical for achieving both.

Referrals are some of the most valuable leads you can get in business. Referral sales require almost no financial investment, but they bring in very valuable warm leads. Once you prioritize turning customers into referral agents and teaching your team members how to make it happen, you will see your business grow. Build strong habits, and it will revolutionize your company.

As part of the Strategic Advisor Board, Mike helps you develop customers into referral agents. Client satisfaction is key to marketing and to business, but inspiring those clients to refer your business to their friends and family will help you to scale and grow. The Strategic Advisor Board will help you to understand how to develop a successful business model, including the implementation of tools, plans, and support structures, as well as how to achieve your organization's optimal potential. Once those steps are achieved, the SAB will guide you in the referral process and how to persuade potential clients that you're the answer to all their problems.

The Strategic Advisor Board is here to help you navigate the multifaceted and complex challenges that obstruct you from scaling your business. Growing a business quickly requires special attention to customers' needs, wants, and desires. With Mike's extensive background in developing a good customer acquisition process, you will have the resources and support to focus on developing products and communication practices that will fill customer gaps and grow your company.

By employing the help of the Strategic Advisor Board and Mike's expertise, your business is guaranteed to expand its reach. By targeting the needs of certain markets and creating relationships with clients that continually add value, you can create a competitive advantage. Your new and improved form of brand cultivation will gain attention, making clients recognize and remember your business. In engaging the SAB's professional knowledge, you will surpass the superficial client relationships your competitors have, and you will build a deep, trusting, long-lasting relationship with your clients that will keep them coming back and referring you to their friends, family, and network connections. Your impact will increase exponentially from where it was before you enlisted the help of the Strategic Advisor Board.

The SAB focuses on smart business growth in a changing environment, concentrating on the customer and helping clients execute strategies as fast as possible. Growing a business quickly requires special attention and focus on the customer's needs, wants, and desires. This means focusing on the problems to be solved that allow you as a business owner to offer a product that fills a gap in the marketplace as soon as possible. Doing this means higher profits in your business, as well as higher rates of customer acquisition and customer retainability. The faster you can develop products that fill these consumer gaps, the more your company will grow. This requires fast action in a rapid production mode to get ahead of your competition.

One of the Strategic Advisor Board's most important factors for success is working with your team of professionals to create a sustainable plan to grow your company. It is important that your vision is executed in your company; however, this cannot happen if your staff isn't able to collaborate together to put your vision into motion. This is why it's so vital to create the procedures and functions within your organization to guarantee execution and success.

9

CULTURE

About

What exactly is company culture? How can it make you money? Will Black understands the importance of both. Take his company, Sharing the Credit's motto, for instance: Doing good is good business. Gone are the days when your product or service was the only thing your customers (and your employees) looked at to deem you a credible business worth spending their time and money on. Your customers want to know the details of how you do business, from how you treat your employees to how you delegate bonuses to what impact you have in your community. While the term "charitable" can be used as a surface level, ingenuine marketing tactic, give it time, and your customers will see right through you. The same can be said about company culture. You cannot just talk the talk with this one. Great company culture is the way to retain and recruit great employees and large dollar signs; it's the way you do business well.

Will Black specializes in merchant and nonprofit funding. Black, CEO and Chief Funding Officer of Sharing the Credit, and Director and Vice President of Finance of the Strategic Advisor Board (SAB), knows the ins and outs of how businesses suffer headaches and financial damage from their company's most needful operation: getting paid in plastic. He has spent three decades in the industry working with hospitals, the military, and every kind of business, from the smallest of start-ups to multimillion-dollar operations. He regularly cuts through the red tape and jargon and shows other CEOs and college business classes how companies get overcharged and how they can avoid it. Black is also well-versed in showing nonprofits how they can secure funding from the businesses that already support them by redirecting built-in fees. The result? Long-term, sustainable funding for nonprofits and dollars saved and shared for for-profits. Black has given away over $1,000,000 and aspires to reach more than $10,000,000. Most impressively: Each donated dollar is unrestricted funding.

Black's passion for people and charities is illustrated through his company, Sharing the Credit, which works with nonprofits and their donor companies, and regularly trains nonprofits and their development staff in the secret knowledge of merchant accounts, as well as the boards he sits on. Those boards include Coastal Jail Ministry, Black's local Rotary, Thrivent, and his church. He is the author of *Paid in Plastic: The Art of the Steal*, which trains business owners how to do a month's worth of math in 30 seconds. He has also written for several business periodicals and has been published online through TheArtofManliness.com. Most notably, Will and his wife, Jill, are the parents of two good-looking children and live in the heart of Savannah, Georgia.

If you need help with cutting costs while donating to your favorite cause with "found" money, Will and his team can get you there.

Defined Culture

In order to drive your revenue, you need to first figure out what car you are driving. As cliche as this may sound, there is validity to knowing what you are working with. A company's culture is outlined by its core values, mission statement, and overall "story." Think about these pieces in your business. How is your culture defined? Is it by serving others? Bettering the community? Solving a need? Providing a service? It is crucial to narrow down your niche so your customers and employees know your vision. It is important that you know your vision because, from it, everything flows.

Your work atmosphere, for one, stems from your defined culture. Consider your vision and values as they would be described to a new employee who is being onboarded. What would they understand about the things you prioritize? Growth? Teamwork? Shared values? Performance? From this relatively objective perspective is how you should begin to analyze the foundation of what the Strategic Advisor Board is referencing as "company culture."

Your vision, mission, and values help create unity within your organization because it sets your company up to work toward the same goal, to head in the same direction. Creating a work culture that aligns with your employees' values is also key to cultivating loyalty and inspiration within your organization.

In other words, you ultimately want to build a business that rallies your workers because you support the things that they care about, both inside and outside of work. This fusion of your company's values and your employees' values will cultivate meaning in the seemingly mundane tasks and create excitement in the everyday meetings and brainstorming sessions.

Your vision, for one, needs to be broad enough to put big goals on the board for you and your employees and specific enough to keep everyone focused. Big goals can be numerical, but they need to create significance too. You can see how quickly culture can become muddled if a company's vision, mission, and values are not clearly defined. Imagine being in the position of a new hire who was told that the organization they are going to work within has a mission statement centered around fighting hunger in their community—which they, too, value—but then comes to realize after months of working there, the organization satisfies that mission statement by giving a small portion of their sales to a local food bank, but no other aspect of the organization seems to be centered around fighting hunger. If you are that individual who is passionate about the issue of ending hunger in the community, you may be disappointed—perhaps to the point of resigning—if that vision was not effectively communicated and defined. The same can be said about the dangers of not marketing your vision clearly to your customers (something that could be costing you big time).

However, regardless of how you define your company's culture, it is established by the people who make up your business. People, whether at home or at work, have needs that need to be met in order for them to perform their best. These needs are best identified by Abraham Maslow's Hierarchy of Needs. This pyramid diagram details what needs humans have that must be met before ascending to the next level of the pyramid. From bottom to top, they are in this order: physiological needs (food, water, shelter), safety needs, belongingness and love, esteem needs, and self-actualization (full potential). Physiological and safety needs are often referred to as basic needs, belongingness and love and esteem as psychological needs, and self-actualization as self-fulfillment needs. This is a helpful tool when addressing, defining, and even repairing your business culture because there is an order to people's behavior. If your employees do not feel safe and comfortable in their place of work or they are underpaid and stressed about paying their bills, they will never be motivated to be creative during your brainstorming sessions.

Before moving forward, you need to consider if you are meeting your staff's basic needs. Some basic needs you may not think of off the top of your head include a healthy work-life balance. Are your employees working tirelessly? Do you encourage breaks and periods of time they do not need to respond to emails and other work tasks? If your employees are burnt out, do not be surprised when your overall company culture is tense, overwhelmed, and underperforming. Do your employees have a sense of job security? Are you demanding of your employees and react with a hot temper when they do not perform and threaten their position? If so, from a psychological standpoint, they will not be in a space to perform their best and, thus, contribute to the positive work culture that results in increased revenue.

Is your staff being challenged and encouraged to grow and work independently, or are you micromanaging them? Is there freedom and flexibility in their tasks and how they choose to accomplish them? Do your employees seem stuck in their positions, or are they heading toward advancement? At every stage of gauging your company culture, you need to be evaluating and reevaluating how you meet the needs of your employees.

Demonstrated Culture

For every reason, make sure your vision, mission, and values are clear and stick to them. Maintaining a cooperative approach helps define your company's culture and sets the stage for success. It is key that your employees understand what your company goals are and the part they play to achieve them. There are parts of your company's culture, though, that cannot just be verbalized in a mission statement; they need to be modeled.

Leadership can make or break company culture. There are the lucky few of us that have not had to live through the experience of working that job with that awful boss. There are also those of us that have worked for organizations with world-class leadership. Leadership can look like a lot of different things to a lot of different organizations, but few people remember much other than how you made them feel. Leaders that understand their limits and embrace the strengths that their employees bring to the table are often the leaders people gravitate toward. The boss that made you feel like you were hardly worthy of being in their presence? Not so much.

Leadership can look like many things, but terms of how it affects company culture vary at each level. For instance, company-wide decision-making leaders will demonstrate culture through the strategies, principles, and processes they implement and enforce. At this stage, it is pivotal that the decisions made by leaders are in line with defined culture. Your employees are looking to see if you are willing to put the rubber to the road when it comes to follow-through. This includes how decision-making leaders charge department leaders to encourage those within their department to be on board with those decisions, reminding them of the collective goal at hand.

More than authority, you need to meet your employees' psychological needs (belongingness and love, and esteem) according to Maslow's Hierarchy of Needs, as previously mentioned. These needs are met in the context of relationships. Regular one-on-one meetings, even if they are brief, place positive deposits into your professional business relationships with your staff. This is a great opportunity to support your staff. Making a point to encourage, praise, and appreciate your employees around each other is another way to meet the psychological needs of those you work with and thus, positively impact your work atmosphere. Your company's culture, to some degree, is impacted by everything that happens in your business, but it's most sensitive to how culture is modeled—especially by those in positions of leadership.

Leadership needs to be the pursuing party in cultivating healthy, professional relationships that result in a great company culture, but they are not the determining factor. Someone could have a great boss but awful coworkers. This all-too-common scenario must be avoided in order to cultivate the great work culture that results in increased dollars. For this reason, you need to knuckle down on your conflict resolution processes. Ineffective conflict management ultimately leads to stressed employees, strained work relationships, poor work performance, and a lack of desire to produce high-level work. Conflict resolution management needs to exist at all levels (employee to employee and employee to authority).

Again, culture is a sort of domino effect. One block falls, and they all could. Conflict is normal and can be a healthy, growing opportunity to deepen work relationships, increase company loyalty and individual productivity, and lots of other positive, revenue-increasing variables. One of the main sources of conflict, arguably inside and outside of a work environment, is unmet and/or uncommunicated expectations. Set the standard for high-level performance up-front, establish clear job descriptions and tasks, and encourage frequent self-evaluation.

Defining your culture with significant values and demonstrating that culture in the way you communicate is also critical. Whether surrounding conflict or a casual check-in at the coffee station, encourage an atmosphere of openness, honesty, and care with your communication. Doing so will encourage membership—a key factor to retaining and recruiting talent. Do your employees feel like they can joke, laugh, and have fun while working? Is gossip regularly occurring? Communication shapes an atmosphere; if it builds your staff's need for esteem (according to Maslow's Hierarchy of needs), then you are on your way to success. If it tears them down? Well, then it tears you down.

Delegated Culture

Your people are the backbone of your business and the foundation of your success. Investing in your leaders and employees will always result in a plentiful harvest. You can clearly define your business culture and do a great job demonstrating what that looks like at the corporate level, but culture that is not expressed and enjoyed by your junior staff will not result in increased revenue.

Just as word-of-mouth reviews and referrals are extremely valuable to you, so should your employee's review of your company's culture. Your employees need to feel a sense of ownership in generating a positive work culture. This does not happen overnight. The employees that feel like they are part of a team, working toward a greater good, are more likely to perform their best, go above and beyond their job description, engage in company events, and be fulfilled and satisfied by the work they do. These positive feelings, when expressed company-wide, result in intangible but also invaluable impact.

Your employees expect just as much from you as you do from them. Appreciating the value that they bring to your company is the first step in cultivating a great team. Good team members impact the culture of your business in many positive ways. For one, a well-functioning team suppresses egos. No one person gets to run the show; rather, a collective effort results in success for all. Team membership also fosters an environment of respect, ethical and supportive communication, participative leadership, equality, diversity, and empowerment to do great work. A high-functioning team that communicates well, cares for its members, feels supported and empowered by its leaders, and works to achieve the same goals will grow your business like a self-sustaining greenhouse grows your plants—invest now, sit back, and relax while your business works for you. Better yet? Your business will actually *enjoy* working for you.

Employee retention is one gain you would achieve with a positive business culture. People who enjoy being at work will stay there. People who do not like being at work will find another job. Employee retention is extremely important if you are interested in making and saving money. On average, companies in 2020 spent over $1,000 on training costs per employee (Elm Learning; March 12, 2021). That time, money, knowledge, and productivity will go down the drain if they decide to leave before they invest back into your business.

While each situation is subjective and affected by numerous variables, building an enjoyable business culture from the ground up can lower your employee turnover significantly, which ultimately saves you money. A difficult work atmosphere will also result in revenue loss from things like increased absences, a higher risk of work accidents and errors, and possibly even increased medical claims. Retaining your employees is also important to cultivate that great team-oriented environment previously mentioned. If a new person is coming onto the team every other week, it may begin to affect overall effectiveness and productivity.

With that being said, minor turnover is, to some degree, inevitable, and laying a healthy foundation will generate an inclusive, flexible, adaptable atmosphere to welcome new, onboarding talent. No one wants to work at a cliché office. Recruiting new employees with a wide range of skills and backgrounds is equally as important as retaining the talent you have. The way your current staff speaks of your work culture will undoubtedly affect the new talent you acquire. Likewise, so will the opportunities your company provides for growth and opportunity. Delegating culture from the ground up means you are generating unity at every point. Do you want your employees to work harder for you? They better know you are working hard for them. Quarterly reviews are a great way to do a pulse check on your business's culture from those you have delegated tasks to. This is also a great time to reinforce your defined culture, ask for feedback about how you can better demonstrate culture from your position of authority, and strengthen your professional relationships.

Distinguished Culture

Remember that self-sustaining greenhouse we mentioned? That is how your business can work for you if your work culture is distinguished. Think of the Fortune 500 companies that are known for their incredible work culture (i.e., Google, Airbnb, etc.). Part of the appeal for working for these companies is the fact that people actually like their jobs. Creating a work culture that people talk about is not the goal, though. The goal (and the reason why you're probably reading this book) is to grow and scale your business, and investing in your business's culture is a surefire way to do so.

That is because your culture is your brand. Your customers may only see your defined culture at first glance, but your employees know your culture intimately. While your staff may not be your primary customer, your bottom line is still impacted. If your staff's basic and psychological needs are not being met, they cannot access the level of self-actualization described in Maslow's Hierarchy of Needs that bears the type of creative, productive, engaged fruit that your business is desperate for. If you are so focused on micromanaging your employees because they do not feel appreciated, challenged/working toward personal growth and advancement, valued, or respected, then you will not be able to focus on selling your product, serving your customers, etc.

Hold your culture to high standards. From your vision and values, work environment, practices, and people—be transparent, be accountable, be integral, gain your employees' trust and motivation. Safeguard your culture. Protect it from becoming toxic, unfair, purposeless, disagreeable, and morally compromising. A stressful work environment will cost you more money than your other efforts to increase your revenue will make you money. Exceed your staff's basic needs and get them to the sweet spot where they feel free to be the best versions of themselves and truly prove to you why you hired them. When your employees feel good, they will work great. When your employees like coming to work, they will do more than just show up; they will make you money.

10
MINDSET

About

Chris O'Byrne is the founder and CEO of JETLAUNCH Publishing. He is a USA Today bestselling author and an expert at book marketing. He was a chemical engineer for ten years in the pulp and paper industry, then started a charter high school where he was both the lead science and math teacher plus the president of the board.

Chris started JETLAUNCH Publishing over 12 years ago and has grown it into a successful company that has served over 10,000 authors. He also has over 100 profitable partnerships in various industries and verticals.

Chris has five children, ten grandchildren, and lives in southeastern Arizona. He has played bluegrass guitar and mandolin for almost 50 years and loves traveling the western US, meeting new people, and camping everywhere he can. He is also an avid birder and reads voraciously.

What is Mindset?

Your mindset is a set of beliefs that shape how you make sense of the world and yourself. It influences how you think, feel, and behave in any given situation. As a business professional, mindset is vital when it comes to achieving goals. Achieving goals is as much a mental battle as a physical one. You need a clear, compelling goal, the willpower to follow through with action, and an unshakeable belief in your own ability to achieve your goals. This is where mindset comes in.

There are two types of mindsets: fixed and growth. Those with a fixed mindset believe their abilities are fixed traits and, therefore, cannot be changed. These people feel that your character, creativity, intelligence, and performance are predetermined and unchanging. They might also believe that their talent and intelligence alone leads to success, and effort is not required. People who have a fixed mindset rely on consistently getting positive feedback and validation to reinforce their self-belief, so they tend to stay within their area of expertise or ability, where they can prove themselves over and over again. They expect certain things to come easily to them, and if something does not come easily, they will give up quickly, assuming that it is outside their skill set.

On the other hand, those with a growth mindset believe their talents and abilities can be developed over time through effort and persistence. With consistent effort, their qualities can be developed and cultivated. They do not necessarily believe that everyone can have incredible talents and abilities just because they try. Instead, they believe everyone can become smarter or more talented if they work hard at it. People with a growth mindset view failure as useful feedback to help them stretch and grow. They look for opportunities to continue learning and developing new skills.

Mindset is distinctive from mindfulness, but the two can complement each other. Your mindset, or the way you approach others, affects your team members. Imagine the difference between a leader that thinks your skill set is predetermined and a leader who encourages you to improve. Mindfulness, or your relationship with your own awareness, can inspire a state of alert, focused relaxation that allows your mind to focus on the present. In short, mindset is your way of thinking, and mindfulness is your relationship with your own thinking.

Do the beliefs of those with a fixed mindset sound like you? Do you find yourself being limited by it and tired of being trapped in your skill set? With the help of SAB, you and your team will be flourishing in your new mindset. Soon, you will be reaping the benefits that come from your willingness to step out of your comfort zone and grow.

Your mindset plays a critical role in how you cope with life's challenges. In the face of setbacks, business professionals with a growth mindset view failure as an opportunity to learn and grow rather than give up. To develop a growth mindset, follow these four simple tips.

First, focus on the journey. An important factor when building a growth mindset is seeing why your journey is valuable; what you are learning and how you are helping others is important to your being. When you're fixated on the end results, you miss out on all the things you could be learning and the opportunities you could be gaining along the way.

Second, incorporate "yet." You can't do this... yet. You're not gaining clients... yet. You are not earning money... yet. If you are struggling with a task, remind yourself that you have not mastered it "yet." Integrating this word into your vocabulary signals that despite any struggles, you can overcome anything.

Third, celebrate effort, not talent. Our culture and media tend to glorify natural talent. Society loves an overnight success story. Remember that there is no such thing as an overnight success, only hard work and determination. When speaking to yourself and your team, change your language. Instead of praising talents, praise the effort you or your team member puts in to accomplish a task. It implies success is due to effort and the strategy employed, both of which can be improved over time.

Finally, take on challenges. Making mistakes is one of the best ways to learn. If you do not try new things because you are scared to fail, you will be trapped in a fixed mindset forever. Instead of shying away from challenges and new opportunities, embrace them.

By using these simple tips in your everyday life, how you think, feel, and behave in any given situation will be changed for the better. With a growth mindset, you and your team will be achieving goals in no time. Remember, achieving goals is as much a mental battle as a physical one. You need a clear, compelling goal, the willpower to follow through with action, and an unshakeable belief in your team's and your own ability to achieve your goals.

Why Mindset Matters

All leaders have a growth mindset, and all great teams have a leader. The leader influences others to accomplish an objective and directs the group in a cohesive and coherent manner. The leader is vital to the success of the organization.

Your company is not just a business; it is a team. Your team members are just like the members of a sports team: equally committed to a common mission, with collaborative interdependence, diversity in skill, a team identity, and an increased commitment of members to the team. Switching from a fixed mindset to a growth mindset will create a successful team. You will be able to build a group of team members that suppress their egos, cooperate, communicate ethically, and respect others.

Being a leader that participates in the success of your team will bring your team achievement. Change your language. Similar to how you should concentrate on your effort rather than your talent, you should empower your team by focusing on their skills. Concentrate on the hard work your team members have exerted to build their skills and help your team. Furthermore, use supportive communication when speaking to your team. Listen to what is being said rather than immediately offering guidance and advice. Allow them time and space to talk. Show interest by looking at your team members and nodding. Check your understanding by summarizing and repeating back, or ask for clarification. It will create a cooperative environment and an atmosphere of trust and respect.

Furthermore, your mindset affects your team as a system. Communication professionals use an idea called systems theory to describe the interworking parts of an organization. A system is a set of interconnected parts working together to form a whole in the context of a changing environment. There is a unique process of each element and a relationship between the elements in the system.

For example, take the human body. It works perfectly together unless an organ is malfunctioning. The same theory goes for your business. As a leader, you are in charge of the system. Your mindset has everything to do with how your business operates.

Systems theory has three main parts: input, throughput, and output. The leader is in charge of the input. The people hired, the information lent, the energy given, and the environment provided is all the input given to the system. Throughput is the process of the group transforming input to output. The roles team members take on, encouragement, and their accomplishments are all throughput. Output is the result of the group's throughput processes. If the leader has a negative mindset, the input and throughput of the system will be negatively affected, leading to a less than optimal output.

Systems also have elements. The first element is the ripple effect: a chain reaction that spreads across the system. One stimulus creates a change in the entire system. This can be negative or positive. The leader yells at one team member, that team member yells at another team member, and it snowballs until the entire team is angry at one another and no one wants to work together. However, if the leader encourages one team member and praises their hard work, that team member will encourage other team members, and the team will want to work together to achieve their goal.

Another element is synergy. The output of group members is superior to the individual efforts of group members. After all, there's no "I" in team. Group effort will create a much better result than the effort of just one person. Remember: your growth mindset is what will ultimately create this. For synergy to occur, you and your team members must be cooperative and interconnected. The key is assembling the right team of individuals that are greater than the sum of their parts. The leader can't be the only one to have a growth mindset; the team members must have it, too. Create a shared vision, core values, and purpose. Synergy will occur when you and your team members all want to work towards the same goal and have the trust and respect towards one another to accomplish that.

The final element of systems theory is the roles taken on by you and your team members. Roles can be both formal and informal. A formal role, of course, is the position assigned within an organization. Think of the manager, the CEO, the accountant, the secretary. However, informal roles emerge from group interactions. There is an emphasis on function, not position.

There are three types of informal roles. Task roles and maintenance roles are both positive towards achieving synergy in your business and are promoted by a growth mindset. Task roles help move the group toward the main goal. By utilizing a growth mindset and encouraging your team members to put forth effort and improve, your members will fall into these roles naturally. Offering ideas and solutions, seeking information, promoting teamwork, and guiding group discussion are all examples of task roles. Maintenance roles help maintain cohesiveness through a social function. Providing praise and encouragement, relieving group tension, promoting balanced participation, and expressing the feelings of the group are all examples of maintenance roles.

Disruptive roles, the third type of informal role, are negative towards achieving synergy in your business and are promoted by a fixed mindset. In disruptive roles, individual goals are more important than group goals. Examples include the stage hog that monopolizes the conversation, the group deserter, the clown that interferes by joking around, the cynic that predicts failure and finds fault, and the uncooperative and negative influencer.

Task roles and maintenance roles should be encouraged and praised. Disruptive roles, however, need to be managed. To stop disruptive behavior, be steady, consistent, and firm. Acknowledge the feelings of the individual. Remember that disruptive behavior is often caused by stress or frustration. For this reason, address the disruption individually, respectfully, and immediately. Be specific about the behavior that is disruptive and set limits. Do not use a fixed mindset toward this individual; they can improve and become better. Help them develop a growth mindset just like you have.

Managing disruptive behavior goes hand in hand with conflict resolution. Conflict is inevitable in the workplace. It is a normal part of all relationships, including the relationships your team members have with each other. Someone with a fixed mindset will look at conflict and view it as destructive. At least one party, maybe both, will lose, and feelings will be hurt. However, someone with a growth mindset will look at conflict as constructive, necessary, and inevitable. With conflict can be found a new approach to an organizational challenge, new ideas, innovation, and creativity. Learning how to manage conflict will determine if it is destructive or constructive.

When resolving conflict, you must intervene in a dispute in order for it to resolve, aim for a conclusion, clarify the norms and processes of the organization, and make a decision that is in the best interest of the organization. The best leaders show empathy: understand and share the feelings of your team members in the conflict. Ask your team members how they are feeling; by inviting someone to open up and share, you show that you think the person is important, and you validate their feelings. Nothing is worse than a boss that tells you to just suck it up and get over it. As a leader, you need to adapt to different situations and conflicts, adapt to a variety of employee needs, and protect the reputation of your team members. Ultimately, listen to all parties, collaborate to reach an agreement and develop a plan, and most importantly, follow through on the plan.

As mentioned before, mindfulness can act as a complement to a growth mindset. Mindfulness is the ability to become aware of how identified or attached you are with your thoughts and perspectives. By focusing mentally on developing a growth mindset, you are using mindfulness. When you are mindful, you begin to see that your imaginary thoughts are false productions of the mind, rather than believing that your thoughts are a true reflection of reality. When you shift your attention away from a constant preoccupation and identification with thoughts, mindfulness can reduce mental stress and increase focus and performance.

Mindfulness in the workplace means nonjudgmentally approaching your work and relations with other team members. An example of mindfulness is closely paying attention, nonjudgmentally, in a meeting and focusing on whatever the presenter is talking about, rather than resentfully wondering when the meeting will end and what to cook for dinner.

Mindfulness has multiple benefits for businesses. It is thought to affect response flexibility, decrease rumination, increase empathy, self-determination, persistence, and enjoyment of work, as well as improve working memory and task commitment. Improved social relationships, resilience, performance, intuition, as well as decreased chronic stress, are all found when workplaces practice mindfulness.

To promote mindfulness at work, practice short mindful exercises with your team members. Be clear about the purpose for introducing mindfulness and to decide what part of the business strategy will handle it, like a well-being program or a cultural shift. Focus, as well, on the benefits of mindfulness and particularly what your organization will gain. First, encourage only doing one task at a time. Multitasking is inefficient because your brain lacks the capacity to perform both tasks simultaneously. Second, slowing down and reflecting on the task at hand can help workers become more efficient, productive, happier, and healthier at work. Despite it seeming counterintuitive, slowing down will help you and your team members become more productive and efficient. Third, accept what cannot be changed at work. Accepting mistakes can reduce unhelpful ways of dealing with perceived failure, like denial or avoidance. Reflect on your mistake and learn from it. Finally, to practice mindfulness at work, adopt a growth mindset.

Everything has come full circle. The Strategic Advisor Board helps you face your limitations, shift your mindset, and empower your team to achieve greatness and success. The Strategic Advisor Board will help you to develop a growth mindset to increase business productivity and lower stress levels, as well as to attain synergy and cooperation among your team members. Once those steps are achieved, the SAB will guide you in proving to your clients that your mindset makes you the best business for them.

The Strategic Advisor Board is here to help you navigate the multifaceted and complex challenges that obstruct you from scaling your business. Growing a business quickly requires special attention to customers' needs, wants, and desires. With SAB's extensive background in leadership and organizational transformation, you will have the resources and support to focus on developing products and communication practices that will fill customer gaps and grow your company.

By employing the help of the Strategic Advisor Board, your business is guaranteed to expand its reach. By targeting the needs of certain markets and creating relationships with clients that continually add value, you can create a competitive advantage. Your new and improved form of brand cultivation will gain attention, making clients recognize and remember your business. In engaging the SAB's professional knowledge, you will surpass the superficial client relationships your competitors have, and you will build a deep, trusting, long-lasting relationship with your clients that will keep them coming back and referring you to their friends, family, and network connections. Your impact will increase exponentially from where it was before you enlisted the help of the Strategic Advisor Board.

CONCLUSION

Deciding to work with the ten CEOs of the Strategic Advisor Board will undoubtedly help you and your business thrive. As a successful business owner, sometimes it's hard to know what you need to grow and scale your business.

As the CEO of the SAB, and other companies, Jason Miller is equipped to help you be the best leader for your business. The impact you have will increase exponentially thanks to the efficient systems and execution standards implemented by unique growth and scaling strategies.

In an age where everyone and everything is online, it is crucial to understand your target audience and create client traffic. With Shelby Long's help, you can develop a unique communication strategy that will create lasting relationships that will continuously and quickly add value to your business.

Michael Sipe specializes in creating expansion with an abundance mindset and in fostering a workforce that is engaged, enthusiastic, and profitable. If you're looking for creative and innovative solutions to improve your business, Michael's three-part process creates solutions to address the most significant challenges to business scalability.

It can be difficult to create and cultivate connections for your business, but Kara James can help you develop a successful onboarding process to ensure new hires stay at your company. She can help you create an environment of inclusion and respect, including group development and how to reduce turnover rate. By ensuring you have a successful onboarding process, you can focus on growing your company.

In an ever-changing economy, it can be difficult for businesses to quickly adapt to be successful. Michael Jackson can help businesses develop resilience to outside economic forces by implementing quick adaptation strategies including processes of communication, changing consumer behavior, and reflection. By implementing an adaptation strategy, your business will be prepared for growth and profit.

Communication is the key to all successful businesses. Consistent customer engagement and innovation allows you to create a connection that generates trust—and trust generates sales. Joel Phillips specializes in improving your digital presence and customer messaging so you can better know your customer and your product and also increase your sales.

Every business has the commitment of fulfillment to face. With the help of Joe Trujillo, you will know not only how to implement, but also how to understand your own unique successful fulfillment strategy, including whether to outsource or stay in-house. This helps you retain current clients and allows for new growth.

Growing relationships is key to growing your business. Mike Owens can assist you in turning customers into referral agents. With a successful business model, including the implementation of tools, plans, and support structures already in place, having a successful referral process will help persuade potential clients that you are the answer.

Great company culture is the way to retain and recruit great employees and large dollar signs. Will Black specializes in creating, demonstrating, and delegating a work culture that aligns with your and your employees' values, which cultivates loyalty and inspiration within your organization, allowing for increased productivity and revenue.

CONCLUSION

Growing and scaling your company cannot happen without a growth mindset. Those with a growth mindset believe that their talents and abilities can be developed through consistent effort and persistence. Having a growth mindset comes from mindfulness. With Chris O'Byrne's help, you can adopt a growth mindset and increase your company's success.

Your potential growth is exponential when enlisting the help of the Strategic Advisor Board. With ten current and successful CEOs with different backgrounds working together to find a personalized and unique strategy to grow and scale your business, you're guaranteed to succeed.

The Strategic Advisor Board

The Strategic Advisor Board is a dynamic team that partners with your business to create custom strategies to help you grow your business on multiple levels. We look at the core foundation and systems within your current business to refine approaches, establish cost-saving measures, and ensure your systems are functioning at the highest efficiency and profitability. We add value to your business to place your business in the best position to implement strategies to scale.

We help businesses emerge from the growth to scale. When a small business grows, resources are added, employees are hired to serve more clients, and strength is added to the business within operations. Scaling your business is where you reframe your brand, automate many of your practices, and create strategic partnerships to begin the process to expand your influence in the marketplace. A comprehensive strategy, a team to support your business, and a trusted network of business service providers is what the Strategic Advisor Board offers to help your business grow into an influential brand.

Our multifaceted and dynamic approach to partnering to develop custom strategies to grow and scale your business is unique in the marketplace.

Are you ready to take the next step in your business?

Learn more at www.strategicadvisorboard.com.